35

Cardiovascular Disease and Diet

Cardiovascular Disease and Diet

DON NARDO

LUCENT BOOKS

A part of Gale, Cengage Learning

GALE
CENGAGE Learning

Farmington Hills, Mich • San Francisco • New York • Waterville, Maine
Meriden, Conn • Mason, Ohio • Chicago

LIBRARY OF CONGRESS CATALOGING-IN-PUBLICATION DATA

Nardo, Don, 1947-
   Cardiovascular disease and diet / by Don Nardo.
    pages cm -- (Nutrition and health)
   Includes bibliographical references and index.
   ISBN 978-1-4205-1231-1 (hardcover)
  1. Heart--Diseases--Diet therapy. 2. Heart--Diseases--Nutritional
   aspects. 3. Heart--Diseases--Prevention. I. Title.
   RC684.D5N37 2015
   616.1'20654--dc23
                          2014021714

Lucent Books
27500 Drake Rd.
Farmington Hills, MI 48331

ISBN-13: 978-1-4205-1231-1

Printed in the United States of America
1 2 3 4 5 6 7 18 17 16 15 14

TABLE OF CONTENTS

FOREWORD

Many people today are amazed by the amount of nutrition and health information, often contradictory, that can be found in the media. Television, newspapers, and magazines bombard readers with the latest news and recommendations. Television news programs report on recent scientific studies. The healthy living sections of newspapers and magazines offer information and advice. In addition, electronic media such as websites, blogs, and forums post daily nutrition and health news and recommendations.

This constant stream of information can be confusing. The science behind nutrition and health is constantly evolving. Current research often leads to new ideas and insights. Many times, the latest nutrition studies and health recommendations contradict previous studies or traditional health advice. When the media reports these changes without giving context or explanations, consumers become confused. In a survey by the National Health Council, for example, 68 percent of participants agreed that "when reporting medical and health news, the media often contradict themselves, so I don't know what to believe." In addition, the Food Marketing Institute reported that eight out of ten consumers thought it was likely that nutrition and health experts would have a completely different idea about what foods are healthy within five years. With so much contradictory information, people have difficulty deciding how to apply nutrition and health recommendations to their lives. Students find it difficult to find relevant yet clear and credible information for reports.

Changing recommendations for antioxidant supplements are an example of how confusion can arise. In the 1990s antioxidants such as vitamins C and E and beta-carotene came to the public's attention. Scientists found that people who ate more antioxidant-rich foods had a lower risk of heart disease, cancer, vision loss, and other chronic conditions than those who ate lower amounts. Without waiting for more scientific study, the media and supplement companies quickly spread the word that antioxidants could help fight and prevent disease. They recommended that people take antioxidant supplements and eat fortified foods. When further scientific studies were completed, however, most did not support the initial recommendations. While naturally occurring antioxidants in fruits and vegetables may help prevent a variety of chronic diseases, little scientific evidence proved antioxidant supplements had the same effect. In fact, a study published in the November 2008 *Journal of the American Medical Association* found that supplemental vitamins A and C gave no more heart protection than a placebo. The study's results contradicted the widely publicized recommendation, which led to consumer confusion. This example highlights the importance of context for evaluating nutrition and health news. Understanding a topic's scientific background, interpreting a study's findings, and evaluating news sources are critical skills that help reduce confusion.

Lucent's Nutrition and Health series is designed to help young people sift through the mountain of confusing facts, opinions, and recommendations. Each book contains the most recent, up-to-date information, synthesized and written so that students can understand and think critically about nutrition and health issues. Each volume of the series provides a balanced overview of today's hot-button nutrition and health issues while presenting the latest scientific findings and a discussion of issues surrounding the topic. The series provides young people with tools for evaluating conflicting and ever-changing ideas about nutrition and health. Clear narrative peppered with personal anecdotes, fully documented primary and secondary source quotes, informative sidebars, fact boxes, and statistics are all used to help readers understand these topics and how they affect their bodies and their lives. Each volume includes information about changes in trends over time, political controversies, and international perspectives. Full-color photographs and charts enhance all volumes in the series. The Nutrition and Health series is a valuable resource for young people to understand current topics and make informed choices for themselves.

Myths About Cardiovascular Disease

One day, while getting ready for bed, a forty-five-year-old real estate broker named Barney felt some unusually severe pains in his chest. He immediately assumed he was having a heart attack and, fearing he would be dead within seconds, delivered a heartfelt good-bye to his wife. She wasted no time in rushing him to the hospital. There, the couple received some good news. To their relief, they learned that Barney had not had a heart attack. Instead, the chest pain he experienced was due to a bad case of heartburn. Caused by stomach acid rising up into the chest area, heartburn can in some cases produce pains that mimic those of a heart attack.

Barney was thankful that the pain had not been a sign of his heart giving out. His wife was thankful, too. She worried, though, that the episode had not taught her husband a lesson about taking better care of himself. He was very overweight, smoked, and never exercised, and she cautioned him that sooner or later he might suffer an actual heart attack. Barney's response, based on his recent experience, was to tell her not to worry. He was now convinced that his heart would give him a warning sign in the form of chest pain. As a result, he would have ample time to reach the hospital and get the help he needed.

A Series of Conditions

But Barney was wrong. His assumption that a heart attack would always be preceded by chest pain and that there would be enough time to seek treatment was and continues to be a myth. In fact, it is one of several myths about cardiovascular disease commonly accepted by millions of people around the world.

Cardiovascular disease, sometimes more generally called heart disease, is not a single medical condition or problem. Rather, it consists of a series of conditions that together can lead to serious injury to the heart or the brain. They can even lead to death. One of the leading cardiologists, or heart doctors, in the United States, Sarah Samaan, lists some of the conditions and problems directly related to cardiovascular disease. They include "heart attacks," she says, along with "high blood pressure, abnormal heart rhythms, stroke, atherosclerosis (cholesterol buildup in the blood vessels), and congestive heart failure," a serious weakening of the heart.[1]

Samaan goes on to explain that certain myths about cardiovascular disease have developed over the past century. Moreover, these erroneous beliefs have sometimes had tragic results, as happened in Barney's case. Recall that he was sure that he would experience a warning sign of a heart attack in the form of chest pain. But according to the American Heart Association, that does not always occur. "Although it's common to have chest pain," a fact sheet for the organization states, "a heart attack may cause subtle symptoms. These include shortness of breath, nausea, feeling lightheaded, and pain or discomfort in one or both arms, the jaw, neck or back."[2]

Sure enough, a few years after his scary run-in with heartburn, one day Barney felt lightheaded and a bit short of breath while sitting at his desk at the real estate office. He thought little of it at the time. But less than an hour later, he suddenly collapsed in the throes of a major heart attack. That evening, in the hospital, Barney once again bade his wife farewell. This time, however, it really was good-bye, because he died a few hours later.

Be Vigilant

Of the several other myths about cardiovascular disease, one of the more prevalent is the assumption that it is an illness mainly affecting men. The reality is that, in addition to the many men it does strike, it is the leading cause of death among women in the United States. One difference is that most women who suffer from the disease die around ten years later in life than men do.

Another well-known myth holds that cardiovascular disease is primarily a disease of elderly people, most commonly defined as folks over age sixty-five. Yet reality is quite different, as Samaan explains. "Fully 45 percent of all heart attacks occur before the age of 65," she states.

> And each year, more than twenty-five thousand American men and eight thousand American women under the age of 45 will die from a heart attack. Medical science has made tremendous progress, and heart attacks are not always the death sentence they once were. But although death rates from heart disease are declining overall, they are on the rise for women under 45. At the same time, we are seeing a slower decline in death rates for younger men, when compared to those for older folks, likely due to dangerously unhealthy lifestyle choices.[3]

Samaan's mention of different death rates for men and women is telling. It belies another common myth surrounding cardiovascular disease: that its symptoms are the same for women as they are for men. The truth is that often they are different. Women are much more likely than men, for instance, to experience less dramatic symptoms such as fatigue, nausea, shoulder pain, back pain, and jaw pain in the hours leading up to a heart attack. Also, few men, but many women, who have survived a heart attack report feeling an overall sense of weakness prior to the episode.

Speaking of symptoms, it must be noted that there may be none at all in the lead-up to a heart attack. The Mayo Clinic says, "Sometimes a heart attack is the first sign that there's any problem at all. Half the men and 64 percent of women who've had a heart attack showed no symptoms of heart disease before the attack."[4]

Still another myth some people believe is that cardiovascular disease typically is inherited from one's parents or other older relatives. The fact is, however, that only roughly 15 percent of cases of the disease can be blamed on genetic factors. True, if one's father or mother had heart disease, one's own chances of getting it are higher. But for most people, the illness is not inherited.

The fact that these and other misconceptions about cardiovascular problems still exist among many members of the American public shows that more education about the disease is needed. After all, a great deal is "at stake," as the American Heart Association puts it. "Because there are so many myths and misconceptions about heart disease," the organization states, many Americans "just don't understand they're at risk." It adds, "The most important thing you can do is to accept that you're at risk and then act on that knowledge. Be smart about your lifestyle. Be vigilant about changes in your body and its condition." The reward will surely be "a longer, healthier life."[5]

CHAPTER 1

The Number-One Killer

Shortly before 1:30 P.M., on June 13, 2008, renowned NBC TV news journalist Tim Russert arrived at the offices of the network's Washington, D.C., bureau, where he served as bureau chief. Also, for the past sixteen years he had hosted NBC's hard-hitting news interview program *Meet the Press*, the longest-running television show in history. Having just returned from Italy, where he and his family had celebrated his son's college graduation, Russert was in good spirits. At the age of fifty-eight, he felt as though he was still a fairly young man and looked forward to many more years as a major figure in television news.

But that optimistic future was not in the cards for Tim Russert. A few minutes after entering the bureau, he suddenly collapsed. A coworker saw what was happening and began administering cardiopulmonary resuscitation, or CPR (chest compressions), on him. Meanwhile, someone else dialed 911 and paramedics were dispatched.

At that moment, no one yet knew for sure why Russert had collapsed. But a later examination by the medical examiner showed that over time a fatty substance called plaque had slowly built up on the interior walls of his arteries. Then, on June 13, "for reasons that we will never know," in two medical experts' words, the plaque in a major artery "ruptured, causing a blood clot to form at the site."[6]

Such a clot appears when tiny components of blood called platelets rush to a place where some bleeding is occurring. The platelets rapidly collect at the spot and at the same time stimulate the production of proteins that will help make the blood near the injury thicker and thereby halt the bleeding. This is all well and good if someone cuts his or her finger and wants the bleeding to stop. But on the inside of an artery, the formation of a blood clot can be dangerous because it can partially or even completely block the flow of blood through that vessel. This is what happened to Tim Russert. When the clot obstructed the blood flow inside his artery, his heart stopped its regular contractions. In an instant, that organ ceased sending oxygen-rich blood to the rest of his body.

Doctors know that for a person undergoing such a series of devastating blows to the heart and arteries, the chances of survival can be extremely low. Sure enough, by the time the paramedics arrived at the NBC Washington bureau at 1:44 P.M., it was too late. Although they valiantly tried three times to get Russert's heart going again, they failed. Sadly for the many Americans who knew or admired him, he was dead.

No Guarantee

Doctors have a name for the physical assaults that Tim Russert's heart and arteries endured. The technical, tongue-twisting term they use in medical textbooks is myocardial infarction. But they and everyone else more commonly call such an event a heart attack. Dr. Sarah Samaan offers the following concise definition:

A heart attack occurs when one or more of [the major] arteries get blocked and blood can't reach the heart muscle. The blockage is usually due to an unstable cholesterol plaque within a heart artery that ruptures or cracks. The body treats this as an injury and sends blood platelets to the damaged area to seal it off. This process results in a blood clot forming inside the artery, abruptly blocking blood flow. Without blood and

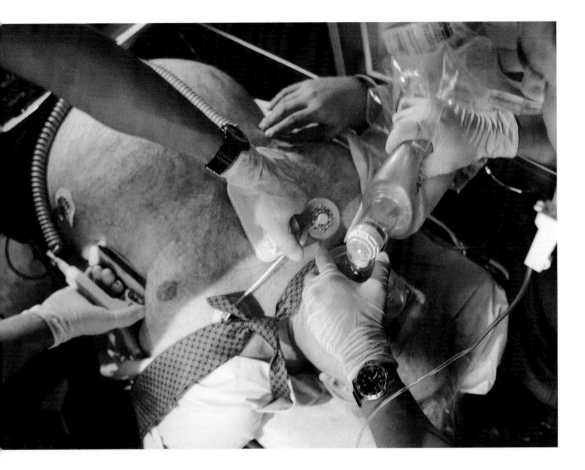

oxygen, the heart tissue literally begins to die and can no longer function normally.[7]

This destructive process is what robbed the nation of Tim Russert's considerable talents. As it turned out, he had already been diagnosed with a form of heart disease. In the year prior to his death, his cardiologist had prescribed medicine and regular exercise, hoping that these measures would keep the condition from worsening. But in retrospect, no one knows whether or not the patient always took his medicine. Nor is it clear that he did the prescribed exercises on a regular basis.

Further complicating matters, even if Russert had followed the doctor's orders to the letter, there was no guarantee that he could have avoided a heart attack. Studies have shown that the disease he had can affect different people in diverse, often complicated ways. As the American Medical Association

Medical personnel use a defibrillator in an attempt to restore a patient's heartbeat.

points out, some risks of contracting heart disease "are within your control, while others are not. The number of risk[s] that affect you may change over the course of your lifetime."[8]

Some Frightening Statistics

It is important to clarify what the American Medical Association means by "heart disease" in this particular case. When used in a general way, that term refers to more than a dozen separate, but often related, medical conditions. For instance, arrhythmia and atrial fibrillation are types of heart disease caused by irregularities in a person's heartbeat. In contrast, cardiomegaly is a condition in which the heart becomes enlarged. Meanwhile, endocarditis is a swelling of the heart's inner lining, and pericarditis occurs when the thin layer of tissue surrounding the heart becomes inflamed.

Tim Russert did not suffer from any of these kinds of heart disease. Rather, the kind that killed him is called cardiovascular disease. Experts frequently refer to it in other ways, among them coronary artery disease (CAD) and coronary heart disease (CHD). Whatever one chooses to call it, it is by far the most common, and certainly one of the more dangerous, forms of heart disease.

In fact, cardiovascular disease, which takes different forms, is the number-one killer of adults in the United States. At any given moment, around 80 million Americans, fully one-third of the adults in the country, suffer from some form of the disease. Also, each year roughly 2 million Americans— an average of one person every thirty-nine seconds—die of cardiovascular disease. Another startling statistic has been reported by the Mayo Clinic, among other leading medical groups: this damaging disease kills more Americans each year than all of the many kinds of cancer combined.

As if that is not bad enough, the World Health Organization (WHO), a branch of the United Nations (UN), has studied the effects of cardiovascular disease worldwide and issued some even more alarming statistics, including the fact that since 2008 more than 17 million people around the world have died from the disease each year. That represents about 30 percent, or three in ten, of all the roughly 55 million global deaths that occurred during each of those years. Moreover, the various forms of cardiovascular disease are on the rise around the world. They claimed almost 2 million more victims in 2011 than they did in the year 2000.[9]

From Life Force to Blood Pump

Yet when one puts the data about cardiovascular disease from recent years aside and looks at its effects over the course of the past few centuries, it immediately becomes clear that this awful carnage is a relatively new phenomenon. Indeed, "before 1900," says Philadelphia's Franklin Institute, "very few people died of heart disease." It was only in the twentieth century that it became "the number one killer."[10] What, then, did people know about the heart and heart disease in past ages? It is even more important to determine why cardiovascular disease was so much rarer in the past than it is today.

Knowledge that the heart is a major organ that serves an important purpose in both humans and animals is much older than most people realize. Some twenty-five thousand years ago, early human hunter-gatherers created vivid, full-color paintings on the walls of caves in western Europe. Among other things, they depicted oversized, reddish-colored hearts within the bodies of the larger beasts they painted, including bison and mammoths. Experts agree that singling out the heart in this manner was no accident. When slaughtering a bison they had hunted and killed, they clearly saw its heart and noted that it was connected to several other parts of the body via a complex network of tubes of varying size.

Although these early humans did not know specifically what the heart does, that complex network must have made the organ seem impressive. The vivid way the cave artists emphasized it in the paintings appears to indicate that they

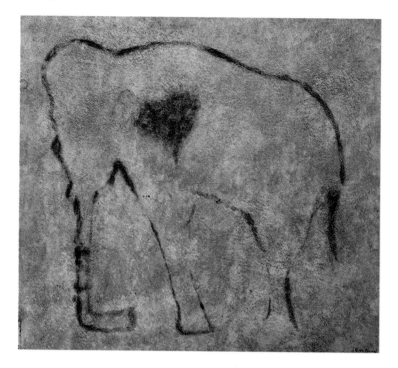

Cave paintings in Spain made twenty-five thousand years ago show that even the earliest humans knew the heart played an important role in life.

equated it with the mysterious force or spirit that made those creatures alive. What is more, some evidence suggests that for these early hunters, eating the hearts of their prey was seen as a special privilege. Perhaps, anthropologist Helen Valborg suggests, "they wished to possess the life spirit of so great a beast." Or it may be that "they wished to assimilate its power and mystery, not merely ingest its flesh."[11]

Skipping ahead about twenty thousand years, ancient Egyptians also depicted the heart in their art. They held that the heart is the seat, or central focus, of humans' life force, as well as the place from which a person's morals spring. These beliefs were reflected in the Egyptians' myths about what happened to people after they died. So important was the heart that the Egyptians believed their gods weighed it before passing final judgment on a person's soul. The purpose of the weighing ceremony was to determine whether the heart's owner was worthy of joining the great master of the afterlife, the deity Osiris, in his subterranean kingdom. If the heart was too heavy—presumably with sin—the unfortunate owner's soul was devoured by a hideous, bloodthirsty creature called Ammut and therefore never made it to the afterlife.

Several centuries later, in the 300s B.C., the noted Greek scholar and thinker Aristotle also concluded that the heart was the body's most crucial organ. In his view, it was the center of vitality, motion, and intelligence. Thus, he viewed the heart, and not the brain, as the hub of human thought and dreams. Additionally, as the source of the heat that the bodies of humans and other mammals generate, Aristotle surmised that the heart must be a hot organ.

The renowned second-century Greek physician Galen agreed with this premise. In his treatise titled *On the Usefulness of the Parts of the Body*, he stated, "The heart is, as it were, the hearthstone and source of the innate heat by which the animal is governed." Galen also provided a physical description of the organ, saying, "The heart is [made of] hard flesh, not easily injured. In hardness, tension, general strength, and resistance to injury, the fibers of the heart far surpass all others, for no other instrument performs such continuous, hard work as the heart."[12]

Galen seems to have grasped that the heart works as a pump. But exactly what it pumped and even why it was designed that way eluded him. He simply did not make what today seems a logical leap to the fact that the heart pumps blood through the arteries, which brings oxygen and other nutrients to the body's various parts.

In fact, no one fully made that critical leap until the seventeenth century. In his groundbreaking 1628 treatise *On the Circulation of the Blood*, English doctor William Harvey penned the twenty-two words that would revolutionize the emerging modern sciences of biology and medicine: "The heart's one role is the transmission of the blood and its propulsion, by means of the arteries, to the extremities everywhere."[13] By "extremities everywhere," Harvey meant all of the body's individual parts, both big and small. Therefore, the gist of his statement was that the heart pumps the blood throughout the body, making life possible.

Enormous Strides

By the beginning of the eighteenth century, Harvey's concept of the heart as the center of the circulatory system had

Two Pumps in One!

Martin S. Lipsky and his fellow doctors who wrote the American Medical Association's manual on preventing heart disease provide this explanation of how the heart pumps blood:

> The four chambers of your heart function as two side-by-side pumps. On the right side, oxygen depleted blood that has circulated through the body passes into the right atrium through two vessels—the superior vena cava and inferior vena cava. The right atrium pushes it into the right ventricle, which moves it into the pulmonary artery to flow into the lungs. In the lungs, the blood is enriched with fresh oxygen. Then the oxygen-rich blood flows through the pulmonary vein into the left side of the heart. The left atrium sends the blood into the left ventricle, which contracts forcefully enough to pump the blood into the aorta, the major artery at the top of the heart. From the aorta, the oxygen-rich blood is distributed throughout the body to nourish cells.

Martin S. Lipsky et al. *American Medical Association Guide to Preventing and Treating Heart Disease.* New York: Wiley and Sons, 2008, p. 6.

become widely accepted in the scientific and medical communities. Also, by the midpoint of that century anatomical descriptions of that vital organ were already fairly accurate. In addition, some physicians had begun to describe and try to treat heart disease. In 1761, Italian researcher Giovanni Morgagni noticed that people with heart problems often had a pronounced "hardening of the arteries," as he called it.[14] This set doctors on the road to understanding the buildup of plaque inside those vessels.

Seven years later, in 1768, English doctor William Heberden made history when he listed most of the symptoms of cardiovascular disease. One of these is a serious pain and squeezing sensation in the chest. He named it *angina*

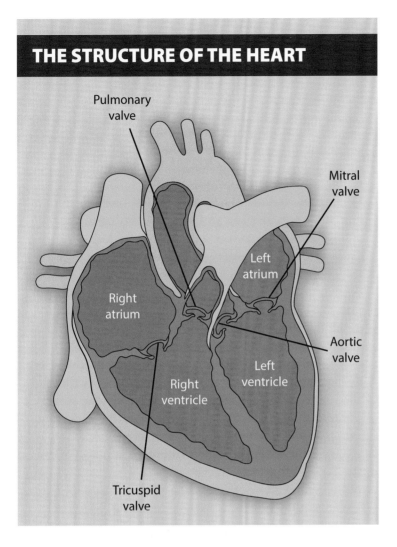

THE STRUCTURE OF THE HEART

Pulmonary valve

Mitral valve

Left atrium

Right atrium

Aortic valve

Left ventricle

Right ventricle

Tricuspid valve

pectoris, Latin for "strangling the chest," a term still employed today. Heberden wrote:

There is a disorder of the breast, marked with strong and peculiar symptoms considerable for the kind of danger belonging to it, and not extremely rare, of which I do not recollect any mention among medical authors. The seat of it, and sense of strangling and anxiety, with which it is attended, may make it not improperly be called angina pectoris. Those, who are afflicted with it, are seized while they are walking and more particularly when they walk soon after eating,

The Doctor Who Dared

Today, operations to treat or correct heart problems occur thousands of time each year in hospitals around the world. All of the doctors and patients involved owe a debt of gratitude to the first modern doctor who dared to operate on a human heart—Robert E. Gross. Born in 1905, Gross attended Harvard Medical School, which calls him "one of the surgical greats of the 20th century, as well as a role model for pediatric surgeons the world over." In August 1938, Gross made history when he corrected a defect in the heart of a seven-year-old girl named Lorraine Sweeney. At that time, the defect she had was considered a death sentence, and most doctors assumed that no child could survive the surgery required to correct it. Against his boss's orders not to operate, the stubborn and courageous Gross did so anyway. Gross would later tell Sweeney that had he failed, his career would have been over and he likely would have become a farmer. Happily, the surgery was a success. Sweeney not only survived her childhood but lived long enough to become a great-grandmother. Meanwhile, Gross went on to make other advances in cardiovascular surgery. When he died in 1988, he left behind an immense legacy: "Children the world over benefitted from the many contributions of this great surgeon, scholar, and teacher. His influence in surgery will long continue through the hands and minds of his many pupils."

"Memorial Minutes: Robert E. Gross." Office for Faculty Affairs, Harvard Medical School and Harvard School of Dental Medicine, 2010. www.fa.hms.harvard.edu /about-our-faculty/memorial-minutes/g/robert-e-gross.

with a painful and most disagreeable sensation in the breast, which seems as if it would take their life away, if it were to increase or to continue.[15]

Heberden was also noted for his strides in treating cardiovascular disease. He was the first person to recognize an effective way of reducing some of the symptoms of the condition. This breakthrough, which occurred in 1772, was based on his experiences with a patient, an elderly man who in his first physical exam displayed angina and some other typical symptoms of cardiovascular disease.

When Heberden examined the man again six months later, however, he noticed that these symptoms had either diminished or disappeared altogether. Hoping to find out why, the doctor questioned the patient thoroughly about his lifestyle and routines. It turned out that the old man had developed a habit of sawing logs by hand for close to an hour every afternoon. Clearly, Heberden deduced, daily exercise helped to reduce some of the effects of heart disease.

Although more advances in understanding and treating cardiovascular disease occurred in the century that followed, most were minor. It was not until the twentieth century that modern medicine started to make rapid, enormous strides in that area. In 1912, for example, it was discovered that plaque itself was not the immediate trigger for a heart attack. Rather,

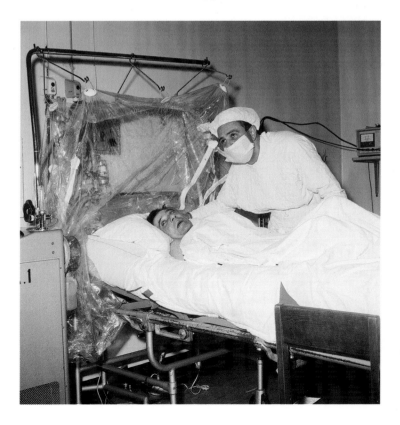

Surgeon Christiaan Barnard stands next to his patient Louis Washkansky on December 3, 1967, in Cape Town, South Africa. Dr. Barnard performed the first heart transplant ever on Mr. Washkansky.

a blood clot that forms inside a plaque-clogged artery sets off such an attack by blocking blood flow.

Another major breakthrough came in 1938 when an American, Dr. Robert E. Gross, performed the first operation to correct a congenital heart defect. The first heart transplant—placing the healthy heart of a person who has just died into the body of someone presently dying of heart disease—was accomplished in 1967 by South African surgeon Christiaan Barnard.

Meanwhile, between 1948 and 1978, the National Heart, Lung, and Blood Institute (then called the National Heart Institute) conducted the first round of its now famous Framingham Heart Study. For thirty years, the study closely monitored the lives and periodically examined the heart and other body parts of 5,209 adults, initially ages thirty to sixty-two. The study revealed the classic risk factors and other facts about cardiovascular disease, making diagnosis and treatment of the ailment far more effective. (The second round of the Framingham Study is ongoing.)

A Growing Epidemic

It was during the twentieth century's astonishingly rapid series of advances that two monumental events relating to heart disease—one very bad, the other very good—took place. The bad one was a significant rise in the incidence of cardiovascular disease around the globe in the first six decades of the century. The rate of increase was especially sharp between the years 1940 and 1967. This prompted the World Health Organization to label it humanity's worst disease epidemic.

The second huge event connected to cardiovascular disease during that era was the global medical community's realization of *why* the rate of that dangerous condition had spiked so spectacularly. A number of separate detailed studies came to the same conclusion: Cardiovascular disease had become much more common because of massive changes in technology and its effects on people's lifestyles. As one author explains it, before the twentieth century:

Most people made their living through some sort of manual labor. Walking was the major means of transportation. Laundry was scrubbed and wrung by hand. Stairs were climbed, carpets were beat, and butter was churned. With the arrival of automation, life became less strenuous. Most manual labor was either replaced or assisted by machinery. Automobiles, washing machines, elevators, and vacuum cleaners became commonplace. Modern conveniences made physical activity unnecessary.[16]

One of the most important and damaging aspects of these sweeping changes in lifestyle was a major transformation of human diets. The phenomenon was especially prominent in developed, or industrialized, nations such as the United States, Great Britain, France, and Germany. Many foods that for centuries had been prepared by hand and eaten in their natural state were now processed by machines. Often these items were stripped of their nutrients and fiber and instead laden with fats and processed sugar. Packaged pastries, such

The surge in obesity and heart disease during the middle of the twentieth century coincides with the increased consumption of processed foods laden with fats and sugar.

as cupcakes and Twinkies; processed cheeses; and highly caloric ice cream became common snacks, as did foods deep-fried in unwholesome oils, including potato chips and french fries.

The unhappy result of consuming too many highly fatty, caloric, low-fiber foods was a stunning rise in weight gain. Obesity (extreme weight gain) and eating disorders also increased, as did the prevalence of mostly useless, fad diets that promised to rid overweight individuals of unwanted pounds. These unhealthy diet-related problems were injurious enough by themselves; when combined with the widespread decrease in physical activity generated by advances in technology, the results were nothing short of disastrous. Millions of people each year found themselves part of the growing epidemic of plaque-clogged arteries, shortness of breath, chest pains, and heart attacks that characterize the number-one killer—cardiovascular disease.

No Longer a Death Sentence?

Physicians and medical researchers also discovered why unhealthy eating habits contributed so much to the expanding epidemic of heart disease. It was because these habits promote obesity, which is a risk factor of the disease—that is, a condition that greatly increases the chances of contracting it. The medical community also found that the lack of physical activity instigated by the onset of the machine age is also a major risk factor for cardiovascular disease. Continuing research identified other common, or classic, risk factors for the disease as well. They include, among others, advancing age, smoking, high blood pressure, diabetes, and having a personal family history of heart problems.

Another important finding that emerged from studies done in the last few decades is that having one or more of these risk factors does not mean a person absolutely *will* develop cardiovascular disease. Indeed, some people display one or more of those factors and never get the disease. Moreover, those individuals who do contract it do not necessarily face a death sentence, as used to be true much of the time. Indeed, experts say that cardiovascular disease can to a large

Effective treatments for cardiovascular disease, such as open-heart surgery and medications, can extend a person's life dramatically.

degree be prevented in the first place by not engaging in the classic risk factors.

Furthermore, even if a person *is* diagnosed with heart disease, several effective treatments now exist, providing that the condition is diagnosed early enough. In the words of two of the world's leading heart specialists, Marc Gillinov and Steven Nissen:

> We will not stand before you like a doctor on *Grey's Anatomy* and offer a solemn pronouncement: "You have six months to live." (We must have missed the day in medical school when the professors explained how to precisely determine a person's life span.) But we do know this: With proper treatment, most heart [disease] patients can maintain a good quality of life and live for years.[17]

CHAPTER 2

Major Causes and Complications

The term cardiovascular disease can refer to several different types of heart or blood vessel problems, including the very common high blood pressure and stroke. But the term is most often used to describe damage to the heart or blood vessels caused by a condition known as atherosclerosis (ath-ur-oh-skluh-ROW-sis). It is a big, complex word with a fairly simple meaning—a hardening of the walls of a person's major arteries. This condition can lead to discomfort, pain, a heart attack, or a number of other complications.

To understand the causes of atherosclerosis and of cardiovascular disease in general, it is first necessary to comprehend exactly how the heart plays the key role in making the circulatory system work. According to Boston Scientific, a leading producer of medical technology, "The heart is the hardest-working muscle in your body." On average, an adult heart is roughly the size of a person's closed fist. Located behind the breastbone, inside the ribcage, that organ pumps about 5 quarts (4.7l) of blood each and every minute of each and every day for its owner's entire lifetime. If that individual lives to be seventy, for example, his or her heart will have beat a total of more than 2.5 billion times. Inside that miraculous pump lie four hollow areas called chambers. These are like separate rooms, each having a door called a valve that allows blood to move in or out. "When you listen to your heartbeat through a stethoscope ('lubb-dubb, lubb-dubb')," Boston Scientific explains, "you hear the sound of your heart valves closing." These "keep blood flowing in one direction through your heart, just like the one-way valves in your home's plumbing. They open to let blood flow through, and then close to prevent blood from flowing back the way it came."[18]

It is important to keep the blood flowing one way because there are two kinds of blood that flow through the body and they are not supposed to mix. Blood containing oxygen and nutrients moves from the heart to the rest of the body through the arteries. After dropping off these items, the nutrient-depleted blood flows back to the heart through the veins.

"Good" and "Bad" in the Blood

Having had a general glimpse of the heart-centered circulatory system, it is necessary to focus in more narrowly on the major arteries. This is because cardiovascular disease is a condition that primarily affects the arteries. Normal, healthy arteries are strong and flexible, like the rubber in a rubber glove. Therefore, the blood flows through them easily, pushing on their walls with a certain amount of force or pressure that doctors refer to as "normal" blood pressure.

Regrettably, for some people certain specific conditions can cause this healthy situation within the major arteries to change for the worse. Over time, various fatty substances can build up along those vessels' inner walls. This process, which makes those vessels thicker and stiffer, is cardiovascular disease's most common form and driver—atherosclerosis.

Medical science has come to recognize several behaviors and conditions that can cause or worsen atherosclerosis and the harmful cardiovascular effects that often result from it. This is why these behaviors and conditions are seen as risk factors for developing cardiovascular disease. One of the most common is a person's intake of excess cholesterol through his or her diet. Cholesterol is a natural waxy, fat-like material that exists in all of the body's cells. The body uses it

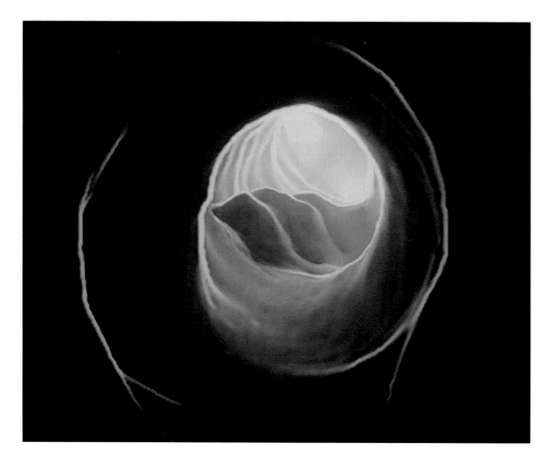

A colored three-dimensional CT scan shows an atheroma plaque (orange, rippled) in the internal carotid artery in the neck.

"to form cell membranes," the American Medical Association points out, "and to make certain hormones, and therefore at healthy levels it is an essential component of cells and blood. Your liver makes as much cholesterol as your body needs—about 1,000 milligrams (mg) per day."[19]

If that naturally occurring cholesterol were the only store of the substance the body ever encountered, life for people everywhere would be less hazardous. The problem, however, is that cholesterol is also found in a number of food items that people regularly consume, including many that are very tasty. Meat, eggs, dairy products, and all the pastries and snacks made from eggs and dairy products contain cholesterol.

Thus, when someone eats those foods, extra supplies of cholesterol enter his or her body and make their way into the bloodstream. There, they move along in small carriers composed of protein, creating tiny individual packages

ATHEROSCLEROSIS

Fatty substances called plaque that build up on the inner walls of the heart's major arteries eventually harden and narrow the artery. When a blood clot occurs in this narrowed space, the flow of oxygen-rich blood to the heart is restricted, causing a heart attack.

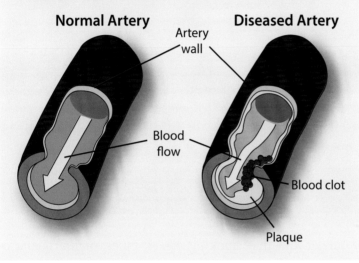

Normal Artery · Diseased Artery · Artery wall · Blood flow · Blood clot · Plaque

called lipoproteins. The two major kinds of lipoproteins are LDL, frequently called the "bad cholesterol," and HDL, the "good cholesterol." The reason they are designated "bad" and "good" is straightforward. HDL is good because it does not contribute to the buildup of fatty plaque on the interiors of arteries; LDL is bad because it *does* contribute to that buildup and thereby promotes atherosclerosis. Sooner or later, that plaque may break open, and if it does, a blood clot may form, leading to a heart attack.

Smoking and Cardiovascular Disease

Another very common risk factor and cause of cardiovascular disease is smoking. It should be noted that the often-repeated notion that only cigarette smoking poses

Smoking adds to the risk of cardiovascular disease by causing artery walls to become rough and blood clots easier to form.

a danger and that smoking cigars, pipes, or marijuana is safe is completely false. It is true that smoking cigarettes is more injurious to the cardiovascular system than smoking cigars, pipes, and marijuana. It is merely a matter of degree, though. Over time, all forms of smoking, including that by people in their teens and twenties, damage the body, including the cardiovascular system.

In whatever manner that one delivers it into the body, the smoke contains chemicals that negatively affect the cardiovascular system in several different ways. First, these substances damage the linings of the arteries, making their surfaces rougher. The rougher they get, the more susceptible they become to collecting plaque, thereby accelerating the formation of atherosclerosis.

Second, exposure to the chemicals in the smoke causes the blood to clot more easily. According to the American Medical Association, "Smoking encourages the formation of blood clots by causing platelets to stick together, which is often part of the cascade of events leading to a heart attack and stroke." Moreover, "some scientists think the blood-clotting effect of smoking is even more important than its role in inducing atherosclerosis."[20]

Third, the smoke reduces the occurrence of HDL, the "good cholesterol," by decreasing levels of certain proteins necessary to HDL's formation. Fourth, smoking can cause blood vessels to constrict, thereby worsening the reduction of blood flow in cases where the arteries are already blocked from deposits of plaque. The British Heart Foundation explains the fifth and sixth ways that smoking hurts the cardiovascular system, stating:

> The carbon monoxide in tobacco smoke reduces the amount of oxygen in your blood. This means your heart has to pump harder to supply the body with the oxygen it needs. [Also] the nicotine in cigarettes stimulates your body to produce adrenaline, which makes your heart beat faster and raises your blood pressure, making your heart work even harder.[21]

Secondhand Smoke

Still another way that smoking damages cardiovascular health is through the effects of secondhand smoke, which consists of the fumes that drift from the burning end of a cigarette, cigar, pipe, or joint. Another kind of secondhand smoke is the smoke that someone who is smoking exhales from his or her lungs. The problem is that secondhand smoke contains the same harmful chemicals that firsthand smoke does. So secondhand smoke can damage the hearts and arteries of people who do not smoke but spend time around active smokers. For this reason, these unfortunate nonsmokers are often called "passive smokers."

Passive smoking is particularly pervasive among children and teens who live with parents or older siblings who smoke. It must be stressed that atherosclerosis is not merely

NUTRITION FACT

1 year

Amount of time needed after quitting smoking to reduce by ½ the risk of developing cardiovascular disease.

a condition that elderly people develop. A young person who smokes regularly, and even a child or teenager who regularly inhales secondhand smoke, can develop early stages of cardiovascular disease. A Harvard Medical School publication explains that:

> At all ages, smoking is the most powerful single contributor to atherosclerosis, and research continues to add to the evidence that exposure to secondhand smoke is also an important culprit. A 2007 study shows that passive smoking is hazardous to children;

Secondhand smoke is especially dangerous for children in households where one or both parents smoke.

Smoking Affects Everyone

To make a rather startling and unsettling point about the dangers of secondhand smoke, cardiologist Sarah Samaan recalls a case study of one of her patients:

> Smoking affects everyone. One patient I will never forget was Patty, a 38-year-old stay-at-home mom with three beautiful children. Patty took low-dose birth control pills. She was not a smoker, but her husband was, and he chose to smoke in their home. Patty came into the E.R. early one morning in the throes of a heart attack, her frantic husband and children at her side. Fortunately, she survived with no long-term damage, and after exhaustive evaluation, the only risk factor we could find was her birth control pills. Combined with exposure to her husband's tobacco smoke, this was a near-lethal mix.

Sarah Samaan. *Best Practices for a Healthy Heart*. New York: The Experiment, 2011, p. 154.

children who had been exposed to environmental smoke during daily life demonstrated significant impairment of their arteries' ability to widen when their tissues needed more blood. Since the subjects were just 11 years old, it's easy to see how continued exposure can lead to illness in early adulthood.[22]

Doctors and other medical professionals see such overwhelming evidence for the connection between smoking and cardiovascular disease that nearly 100 percent of them urge patients, and often relatives and friends, not to smoke. The best approach, they say, is not to start smoking in the first place. But if someone already smokes, he or she should try to quit, and the sooner the better. As cardiologists Marc Gillinov and Steven Nissen point out, "If you quit smoking right now, your arteries will begin to return to normal quickly. Over the next five years, your risk of heart attack will plummet, approaching the same level as that of somebody who has never smoked. It's never too late to do your arteries a favor. Quit now!"[23]

Also, one should try to stay clear of secondhand smoke whenever possible. That means avoiding places where a lot of smoking occurs. In addition, many doctors say, it is perfectly all right for a nonsmoker to ask family members and friends who smoke not to do so in his or her home or car.

High Blood Pressure and Obesity

A third major cause of cardiovascular disease is high blood pressure. It not only contributes to atherosclerosis, but also weakens the heart. First, the extra force or pressure of the moving blood on the arteries' walls can create tiny tears in them, and these soon turn into scar tissue. On a microscopic scale, that scar tissue is jagged. It resembles a latticework with ridges and crevices, and the crevices become places for plaque to cling and collect. As the plaque grows thicker, it can cause one or more arteries to steadily narrow and harden. In turn, over time this makes the heart work harder, which puts it at increased risk of damage by other risk factors associated with cardiovascular disease.

High blood pressure is sometimes called "the silent killer." This is because it usually has no specific symptoms, which means that a person can have it and not experience any warning signs. That is why it is important to have a doctor or nurse check one's blood pressure from time to time. "Many people who look and feel perfectly fit have high blood pressure," the American Medical Association cautions, "while some people who are overweight, smoke, or show other risk factors for heart disease have normal blood pressure. That's why the only way to know for sure if you have high blood pressure is to be tested."[24]

Obesity is another frequent cause of cardiovascular disease. A person is considered to be obese when he or she is at least 20 percent heavier than the weight recommended for people of their height by the medical community. According to one of the leading American medical facilities, the Cleveland Clinic, more than one in three American adults are obese and more than one in twenty adults are extremely

obese. Also, more than one in six children and teenagers in the country are obese.[25]

The overall cause of this alarming situation is that large numbers of Americans are eating more and exercising less. In part, doctors say, this is because of the rise of the fast food industry in the past thirty to forty years. In the words of one expert, "The slow, insidious [menacing] displacement of home cooked and communally shared family meals by the industrial food system has fattened our nation and weakened our family ties."[26]

Indeed, throughout most of the twentieth century, Americans did not eat at restaurants, including fast food ones. But toward the end of the century, eating at restaurants became increasingly common. By 2010, says Mark Hyman, director of the UltraWellness Center, 50 percent of an average family's meals were eaten outside the home. "Research shows that children who have regular meals with their parents do better in every way," Hyman states. That includes a reduction in "the incidence of childhood obesity. In a study on household routines and obesity in U.S. preschool-aged children, it was

Since the 1970s families are eating out more, which means a higher consumption of processed foods. By 2010 only 50 percent of families' meals were home cooked.

shown that kids as young as four have a lower risk of obesity if they eat regular family dinners, have enough sleep, and don't watch TV on weekdays."[27] Other reasons for the recent rise in overweight and obese Americans are more frequent between-meal snacking, especially of high caloric foods, and not getting enough exercise.

Many people have heard that obesity is bad for the heart but are unsure why. Simply put, gaining too much fat, particularly around the waist, puts a person at a higher risk of suffering from high blood pressure, high blood cholesterol, and diabetes—all risk factors for heart problems. More specifically, Dr. Sarah Samaan says:

> Fat that collects around the waist can churn out a toxic mix of hormones and inflammatory substances that have been strongly linked to a higher risk of heart attacks, blood clots, and other health problems. Not only does obesity expose the heart and other organs to these dangerous chemicals, it also requires the heart to work overtime, pumping blood through literally miles of extra capillaries, and may result in measurable changes in the heart's ability to do its work effectively. The heart may become thicker and less elastic. These two factors have been associated with congestive heart failure, a condition that is twice as common in obese individuals as in those of normal weight.[28]

Genetic Risk Factors and Other Complications

In addition to causes of heart disease based on what a person does, for instance smoking or overeating, there are a few that are based on who he or she is. First, cardiovascular disease can have genetic risk factors, meaning it can run in families. The American Medical Association points out that:

> Having parents or siblings with the disease is a major risk factor. But there is no single gene for cardiovascular disease. In fact, geneticists think that more than a thousand separate genes may influence the overall cardiovascular system. There are separate genes for

obesity, high blood pressure, and diabetes, all risk factors for heart disease. Scientists are still identifying these genes and studying how they interact with one another—and with other influences, such as diet—in an individual or a family.[29]

Similarly, women can encounter certain physical problems or complications relating to cardiovascular disease based solely on their gender. First, there is the fact that they can get pregnant, and if a mother-to-be develops a heart condition, it can have harmful effects on the child she is carrying. Also, women who are not pregnant often take birth control pills. By themselves, the pills are not potentially harmful

Actress Elizabeth Banks (left) and TV personality Star Jones promote the 2012 "Go Red for Women" campaign in support of awareness of heart disease in women.

to the heart. Women who both smoke and take the pills, however, run a risk for developing cardiovascular disease.

In addition, many women experience a distinctive psychological or emotional reaction to learning that they have, or might have, cardiovascular disease. They are frequently the principal caregivers in their families and as such can feel like they are letting their husbands, partners, or children down by getting sick. This puts extra stress on those women, which makes their ordeal with heart disease more painful and their recovery more difficult. The Mayo Clinic cites the case of a medical professional named Jeanie. She had no inkling that she was suffering from cardiovascular disease, and one day she displayed signs of an impending heart attack. Jeanie later recalled:

> A nurse told me to go to the ER right away because I was having a heart attack. I thought, "This can't be happening to me, I'm the mom, I can't be sick." I didn't go for several hours. I had to get one son ready for prom and another off to camp. I'm lucky to be alive.[30]

Heart Failure and Other Complications

Whatever the causes of a person's developing cardiovascular disease, he or she may experience one or more painful or life-threatening complications, or outcomes. The most often cited, and certainly one of the most damaging, is a heart attack. But an unknown number of people with the disease never have a heart attack.

Some of those who manage to avoid the path that leads to heart attack instead suffer from a condition that doctors call heart failure. For people unfamiliar with the term, it can be scary. Often they conjure up an image of one's heart suddenly "failing," in the sense of ceasing to beat and bringing on immediate death. However, the medical term "heart failure" does not define "failure" that way. Instead, it means that a person's heart is not presently pumping blood as efficiently

Sudden Cardiac Arrest

Stroke, heart failure, and aneurysms are among the several dangerous complications of cardiovascular disease. Sudden cardiac arrest is another. Sudden cardiac arrest occurs when the heart unexpectedly and abruptly stops beating. Just as suddenly, the person stops breathing and loses consciousness. Most often, this lethal condition happens as the result of an electrical disturbance in the heart that upsets its pumping action. It rarely occurs in a healthy heart and body. Rather, sudden cardiac arrest nearly always strikes someone who already has some sort of heart problem, especially cardiovascular disease. Obviously, sudden cardiac arrest must be treated immediately. If a medical professional or someone else does not restart the heart within a few seconds, death is certain to follow. Appropriately, the technical name for this unfortunate outcome is sudden cardiac death.

as it should. The organ is still beating. But it is "failing" to meet the body's requirement of obtaining oxygen from the blood. Basically, therefore, heart failure is another way of saying "a weakened heart."

Heart failure can result from damage caused by a heart attack, high blood pressure, the onset of a serious disease, an injury, or other means. It is imperative that someone with heart failure see a doctor and receive treatment. Otherwise, the condition is likely to get worse, as this complication of cardiovascular disease has some of its own complications. One is a malfunction of the kidneys that causes the body to retain too much fluid (mostly water). "The resulting increase in circulating fluid," Gillinov and Nissen explain, "causes congestion in the lungs. When this happens, the patient experiences shortness of breath, particularly during exercising or when lying flat in a bed at night. If enough fluid accumulates, the ankles and feet swell, a condition termed edema."[31]

Another serious complication of cardiovascular disease is stroke, a condition that occurs when the normal flow of

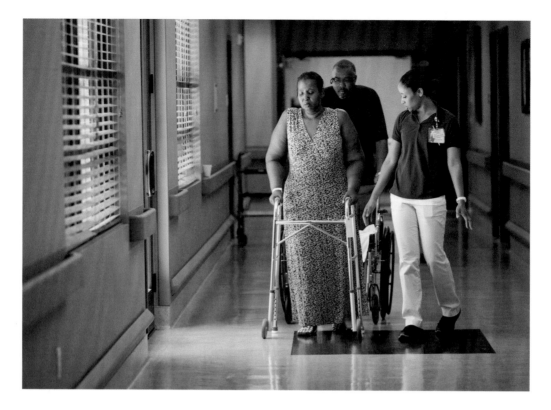

A physical therapist assists a woman recovering from a stroke—a medical emergency that occurs when the normal flow of blood to the brain stops, which can cause damage to motor skills.

blood to the brain stops. In mere minutes, the person's brain cells, which require blood to survive and function, begin to die. In the most common kind of stroke, known as ischemic stroke, the blood flow to the brain slows or stops due to a clot blocking a major blood vessel. Another, rarer version of stroke—hemorrhagic stroke—happens when such a vessel ruptures, causing bleeding inside the brain. The classic symptoms of a stroke include a sudden weakness or numbness in the face or another body part, most often on only one side of the body; having difficulty speaking or understanding what others are saying; feeling dizzy or experiencing a loss of balance, making walking harder; and the onset of a bad headache.

Still another complication of cardiovascular disease can be one of the most deadly. Called an aneurysm, it is a bulge or balloon-like swelling in an artery's wall. If that bulge grows big enough, it can burst, initiating dangerous bleeding and in the worst cases causing death. Aneurysms can appear in arteries located in the chest near the heart, in the brain, or in other parts of the body. An aneurysm that occurs in the brain, called a cerebral aneurysm, almost always brings on a stroke.

Aneurysms, strokes, heart failure, heart attacks, and other complications of cardiovascular disease are plainly serious, dangerous, and often fatal. This explains in the clearest possible terms why that disease is the world's number-one killer. It is essential, therefore, for everyone, young and old alike, to be on the lookout for it by learning its symptoms.

CHAPTER 3

Symptoms and Medical Diagnosis

When she was fifty-three, a North Dakota resident named Mary started to notice an unusual kind of pain she had never experienced before. "When I would walk up stairs, I felt a pain in the middle upper part of my chest," she later recalled. "It radiated into my jaw. I later learned this was called angina, and it meant my heart wasn't getting enough blood. I was also getting headaches. The jaw pain was the worst, though."[32]

Rather than make an appointment with a doctor, Mary ignored these symptoms for three months. When later asked why, she said:

> I felt I was too young. I thought that heart disease was for people in their 60s and 70s. Also, I fell about six years ago and have had back issues ever since. I have one herniated disk and two bulged disks. I felt like this was something I was complaining about a lot and people were tired of hearing about my medical stuff. I felt like I couldn't talk about the chest and jaw pain I was experiencing. I didn't think people wanted to hear about it.[33]

A particularly unusual aspect of Mary's failure to seek a diagnosis—a medical opinion identifying her ailment—was that her own father was a doctor. She explained:

As a kid, we'd be sitting around the table at dinner and he'd get a call from someone saying they'd been sick for three weeks asking him to come examine them in the emergency room. So I've always been timid about going to get checked out for little things. That's what I thought my jaw and chest pain were—a little thing.[34]

Mary's pain was not a little thing, however. When she finally saw a health care professional and described her symptoms, she was scheduled for various medical tests. After following these standard steps of medical diagnosis, her doctor informed her that she had cardiovascular disease. She was lucky, he told her, because if she had waited any longer to seek help, she might well have had a heart attack. Blatant, debilitating symptoms like her jaw pain should never be ignored, he added. His advice is frequently echoed by other

Some people fail to realize the early signs of cardiovascular disease that can be discovered by scheduling regular medical exams.

doctors, along with leading medical institutions. According to the Mayo Clinic, for example:

> You might not be diagnosed with cardiovascular disease until your condition worsens to the point that you have a heart attack, angina, stroke or heart failure. It's important to watch for cardiovascular symptoms and discuss any concerns with your doctor. Cardiovascular disease can sometimes be found early with regular visits to your doctor.[35]

The Classic Symptoms

Mary's pain started "in the middle upper part of my chest." This example of angina is a classic symptom of cardiovascular disease. Typically, a person can also feel mild to moderate pressure or squeezing sensations in the chest that seem to be related to the pain, which in fact they are. That the pain soon migrated to Mary's jaw is also a common sign of cardiovascular disease. Patients often complain of feeling pains in one or both arms, the hands, the stomach, the back, the neck, or the jaw.

Shortness of breath (when someone feels he or she cannot get enough air) is another classic symptom of the disease. This feeling often comes and goes in the early stages and happens more frequently as the person's cardiovascular problems increase in severity. (Shortness of breath is also a symptom of another heart condition, cardiomyopathy, in which the heart's muscular walls become enlarged and rigid.)

There are still other common symptoms of cardiovascular disease. One is increasingly frequent feelings of nausea (queasy feelings in the stomach that may lead to vomiting). Another is feeling lightheaded. A person may also periodically break out in a cold sweat.

It must be emphasized that these symptoms of cardiovascular disease in general can at any moment progress directly into those of a more specific complication of the condition: a heart attack. Quite often, in fact, a heart attack's symptoms are the same as those for the disease itself, only more pronounced, intense, painful, and frightening. The angi-

Mild to moderate pressure or squeezing sensations in the chest is one of the classic symptoms of cardiovascular disease.

na lodges near the center of the chest and becomes acute. Meanwhile, the shortness of breath gets worse and may not go away, while a sharp pain may appear in one or both arms. This progression of the standard symptoms' intensity is exemplified by the case of a woman named Angela, as reported by the U.S. Department of Health and Human Services' Office on Women's Health:

In 1991, I went to the ER with chest pains twice in one week. They said it was ulcers (bleeding in the stomach). Then the pain became very intense. Again, the ER said there was nothing they could do. I refused to leave and was admitted for observation. Later, the doctor on duty saw my EKG [a reading of heart activity taken by a machine] and asked, "Where's the 34-year-old who had the massive heart attack?" I had emergency surgery. But the damage was done. Only part of my heart muscle now functions. I had to quit a job I

loved, and my life is completely changed. They thought
I was too young to have a heart attack.[36]

X-Ray and EKG

Clearly, the medical staff Angela first encountered in the
emergency room did not do their jobs correctly. Perhaps
because they were unusually busy when she arrived, they
gave her only a cursory examination, mistakenly diagnosed
ulcers, and sent her on her way. Only when she insisted on
being admitted were the necessary steps taken to indicate
she suffered from cardiovascular disease.

To arrive at a correct diagnosis, a series of standard diagnostic steps must be followed. The first step should be to
take a medical history. That is, the health care professional
asks a series of detailed questions about the patient's life;
physical well-being; any diseases or other medical conditions
he or she may have had over the years; any recent physical
symptoms that have been bothering him or her; and so forth.
Next, the health care professional listens to the patient's heart
with a stethoscope and checks the patient's blood pressure
to see if it is elevated.

These initial diagnostic steps alone often provide a basic,
preliminary indication of what may be wrong with the
patient. A health care professional will not want to leave
anything to chance, of course, especially when dealing with
a possible case of heart disease. So in almost all cases, the
health care professional will administer one, two, or more
diagnostic tests that will either confirm or disprove the sus-
picions.

Often one of these tests is a chest X-ray (or "chest film").
Though fairly simple, the image of the heart, lungs, and other
parts of the chest captured in the X-ray process can be very
revealing. In that image, the health care professional can see
the heart's silhouette, or outline. Almost at a glance, he or
she can tell if that organ has acquired an odd shape or if it is
bigger than it should be. These are signs that something is
adversely affecting it.

Another common medical test that aids in a diagnosis of
possible heart problems is an electrocardiogram, often called

"Don't Diagnose Yourself!"

When it comes to the symptoms of cardiovascular disease and heart attack, even doctors sometimes do not always pay attention to them as they should. This was proven in a big way by the life-threatening experience of Bryan McIver, a specialist in thyroid cancer. When he was thirty-seven, he worked at the renowned Mayo Clinic in Rochester, Minnesota. One evening after leaving his lab at the clinic, he met some friends for dinner. "During all of that day leading up to the dinner," he later recalled, "I had a kind of niggling [nagging] discomfort. It wasn't really a pain, just discomfort." Fearing he might have some sort of heart problem, McIver performed an informal stress test by running up seven flights of stairs. This made the discomfort go away, so he concluded that all was well. Later that night, however, he collapsed in the throes of a massive heart attack. It was so bad that his doctors were surprised he managed to survive. McIver learned several lessons from the experience. One was that he should have paid heed to the symptoms he had felt leading up to the attack. "You should never ignore symptoms when it involves pain in the chest," he says. "And don't diagnose yourself. I'm a doctor and I didn't get it right!"

Quoted in Mayo Clinic. *Healthy Heart for Life!* New York: Time Home Entertainment, 2012, pp. 154–155.

an EKG or ECG for short. It looks at and records the heart's electrical activity. The Texas Heart Institute explains:

> During the test, you will lie on an examination table. A technician will clean the areas on your body where the electrodes will be placed, usually your chest, back, wrists, and ankles. The electrodes have wires called leads, which hook up to the electrocardiogram machine. Once the electrodes are in place, you will be asked to lie down. The technician will enter some information into the electrocardiogram machine and

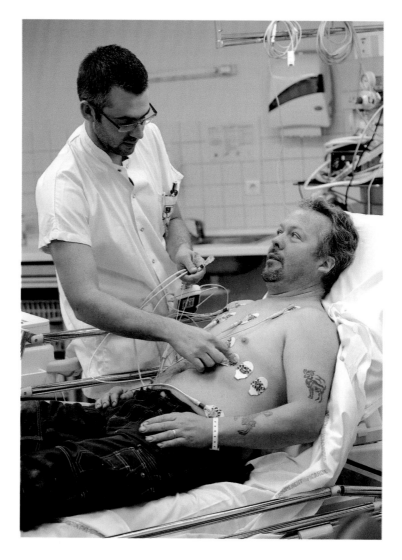

then tell you to lie still for about a minute while the machine takes its readings. The test is completely safe and painless.[37]

The EKG takes advantage of the fact that the heart emits a small electrical signal each time it beats, thereby creating a heartbeat rhythm. The machine is designed to detect whether that rhythm is steady and regular or uneven and irregular. Cardiologists and many other kinds of doctors are trained to recognize what the various heartbeat patterns recorded by the machine mean. For example, such a medical professional knows that one particular pattern is typical of a weakened heart, which will suggest that the patient may be suffering from heart failure. Similarly, another pattern may indicate that the patient is in danger of having a heart attack in the near future.

Stress Test and Angiogram

One of the most effective and useful medical tests employed to diagnose cardiovascular disease is called a stress test. (Some medical professionals call it a treadmill test or exercise tolerance test.) A major reason that medical professionals frequently use it is that some heart problems are easier to detect when the heart is beating fast. To get it to beat fast, the patient performs a round of vigorous exercise, most often by walking on a treadmill or riding a stationary bike.

Dr. Sarah Samaan describes one kind of patient she typically asks to take a stress test. Jesse, she says, is "a 39-year-old gentleman who weighs more than 300 pounds." An insurance broker, he is "diabetic, has high blood pressure and high cholesterol, and worries about the breathlessness he feels when he climbs the stairs to his third-floor apartment. We will schedule a stress test and hope that the results are good."[38] With some exceptions, like Jesse, most people who take a stress test already display some symptoms of cardiovascular disease.

Just before a patient like Jesse begins exercising, a technician hooks him or her up to an EKG machine so that the heart can be monitored during the test. After the patient starts walking or riding, the technician or the doctor increases the degree of difficulty every two or three minutes. This is most often done by increasing the treadmill's or bike's speed. Or else the slope of the machine may increase, making the patient feel as if he or she is traveling uphill.

When the exercise phase of the test is over, the patient is allowed to sit or lie down and rest. Meanwhile, the medical professional examines the EKG readout to look for patterns in the heart's electrical activity. The machine also measures the patient's blood pressure levels during the test to determine if the heart is getting sufficient oxygen. In addition, sometimes during the test a patient will be unable to

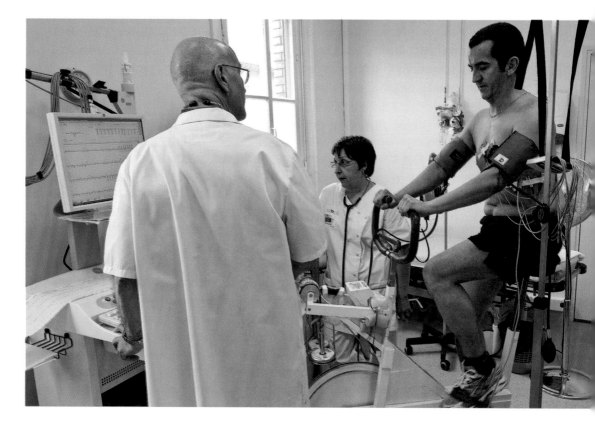

A stress test consists of an EKG performed while the patient is doing a physical activity, such as riding a stationary bicycle, to increase the heart rate.

exercise for the length of time that is normal for a person of that age. In that case, the doctor will know that the patient's heart is not receiving the proper amount of blood flow.

If a patient's stress test results in negative or abnormal results, the doctor may ask him or her to have an angiogram, the technical name of which is coronary angiography. A person may get an angiogram for other reasons as well. If someone already suffers from chest pains and they are getting worse, if a patient has heart failure and the doctor wants to monitor it, or if a person is about to undergo heart surgery, a doctor may ask for him or her to have an angiogram.

An angiogram works by releasing a special dye into the bloodstream in order to make concentrations of plaque and other blockages in the major arteries visible on X-ray pictures. According to Medline Plus, a service of the National Institutes of Health:

> Before the test starts, you will be given a mild sedative to help you relax. An area of your body, usually the arm

or groin [upper thigh], is cleaned and numbed with a local numbing medicine (anesthetic). The cardiologist passes a thin hollow tube, called a catheter, through an artery and carefully moves it up into the heart. X-ray images help the doctor position the catheter. Once the catheter is in place, dye (contrast material) is injected into the catheter. X-ray images are taken to see how the dye moves through the artery. The dye helps highlight any blockages in blood flow. The procedure may last 30 to 60 minutes.[39]

The results of an angiogram may show exactly what the doctor suspected—that one or more of the patient's arteries are blocked by the effects of atherosclerosis. If so, the test will also pinpoint the locations of the blockages, indicate how much blood flow is presently obstructed, and see how blood is moving through the heart and other blood vessels. This data is vital to the doctor because it allows him or her to decide which treatment will be most effective for that particular patient.

CT Scans

In some cases, a doctor attempting to diagnose cardiovascular disease may feel that a chest X-ray, EKG, stress test, and other tests have not produced enough information. If so, he or she may have the patient undergo computed tomography, or a CT scan. Often called by its nickname, a "cat scan," it is an X-ray method that employs a computer to make cross-sectional images of a patient's heart.

This versatile imaging technique allows medical professionals to view the heart's structure and how effectively it pumps blood. A CT scan can also show how much plaque has built up inside an artery and reveal abnormalities in the big blood vessels in the heart's immediate vicinity. In addition, such a scan is often used to detect scarring of the heart muscle caused by a heart attack. (A person with cardiovascular disease can have what he or she thinks is a serious episode of angina and not realize it was actually a mild heart attack. By revealing the telltale scar tissue, a CT scan exposes the truth to both doctor and patient.) What is more, a CT scan measures the amount of calcium in the major arteries. This tells a doctor how much plaque exists in those arteries that has not yet caused the patient any pain or other unpleasant effects.

When a person goes to have a CT scan, he or she sees that the scanner is a big apparatus that features a short, tunnel-like tube in the center. The patient lies face-up on table that slowly slides through that central tube. In the process, the machine takes numerous sophisticated X-ray images of the heart, each image representing a thin layer of the organ. A computer attached to the scanner then assembles the assorted pictures, creating a single highly detailed image.

Studies have shown that the amount of radiation

A patient enters a CT scan machine, which uses X-rays and a computer to create detailed images of the inside of the body and functioning organs.

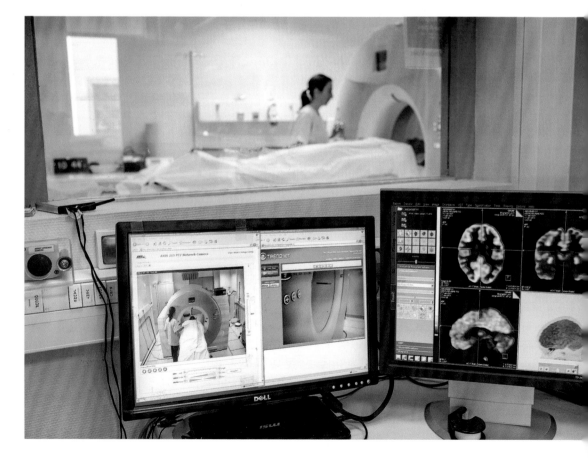

The Gated Blood Pool Scan

Fortunately for people who have symptoms of cardiovascular disease and need an accurate diagnosis, a wide array of reliable medical tests now exists. From older but still dependable ones such as X-rays and electrocardiograms to newer technologies such as high-speed CT scans (Multi-Detector Computed Tomography, or MDCT), these tests examine virtually every conceivable heart function. One such test that few non-medical personnel have ever heard of is the gated blood pool scan. It uses a special dye to show how blood pools in the heart. In particular, it allows a doctor to see if the heart is pumping harder because of the existence of one or more arteries obstructed by atherosclerosis.

During a gated blood pool scan, the dye is injected into the patient's bloodstream and quickly makes red blood cells "visible" to the machine's detectors. Then a special camera takes pictures of those red blood cells moving in and out of the heart. Often this technique is used to confirm the results of other tests that have indicated that one or more arteries may be blocked. One of its advantages is that it is noninvasive, in that no instruments actually touch the heart.

involved in taking a CT scan is quite small. Therefore, the medical community considers it a safe test overall. (One exception is pregnant women, because the radiation dose to which a woman is routinely exposed can be hazardous to the fetus she carries.) Nevertheless, if either the patient or doctor objects to having a scan on account of the radiation, another machine that produces detailed images of the heart, and does so without exposing the patient to radiation, is available.

Having a Cardiac MRI

That device is called an MRI machine. The letters stand for Magnetic Resonance Imaging, and the key word here is magnetic, as the test, which is called a cardiac MRI, utilizes the body's built-in magnetic properties to generate the image. In the words of the Texas Heart Institute:

The MRI machine looks like a long, narrow tube. When you are placed inside of the tube, you are surrounded by a magnetic field. The human body is made up of different elements, most of which are also magnetic. The magnetic field surrounding your body reacts with the magnetic elements within your body to transmit a faint radio signal. For example, your body contains a large amount of hydrogen atoms, and those atoms are very magnetic. The MRI machine's magnetic field excites the hydrogen atoms in your body, which in turn creates a small radio signal. A computer reads

A cardiac MRI shows the heart and the great vessels in a 360-degree view.

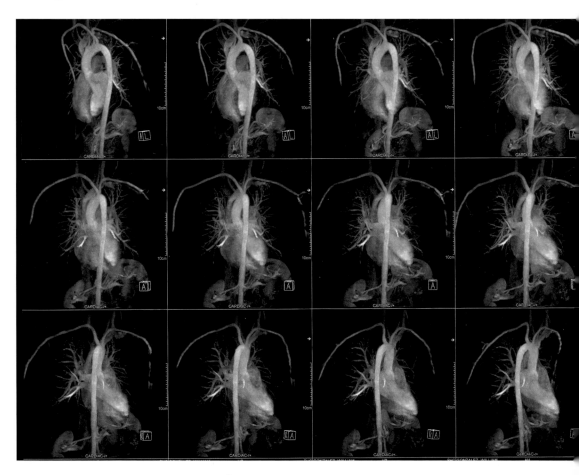

the radio signal and turns it into an image that can be seen on a computer monitor.[40]

The patient's encounter with this unique, highly advanced example of modern medical technology begins when he or she enters the MRI room. Visible in the center is the machine, which has a tube roughly 3 feet (1m) wide in the middle. The technician double-checks to make sure the patient has no metal objects either on or inside the body. This question is extremely important, as the machine's magnet is so powerful that it will violently attract any nearby metal object, very possibly injuring the patient.

As in a CT scan, the patient lies on a table that slides into the tube. That person is given headphones so that when inside he or she can hear outside voices. This is essential because the technician needs to communicate with the patient at key moments during the test. The patient also hears, and in fact cannot miss, the machine itself, which emits a very loud knocking sound when it is taking images. Fortunately, this noise is somewhat muffled by earplugs the patient receives just prior to entering the tube. On average, the test lasts about forty-five minutes to an hour.

When the MRI is complete, the doctor can view both still and moving images of the patient's heart and major blood vessels. On the one hand, the doctor studies the images to confirm or reject a diagnosis of cardiovascular disease or some other suspected heart ailment. On the other, the remarkably clear images aid that physician in choosing an effective treatment. Indeed, at that point, assuming cardiovascular disease has been diagnosed, picking just the right treatment from several viable ones becomes the next order of business for the doctor-patient team.

NUTRITION FACT

42%

Percentage of women who have heart attacks that die within one year, compared to 24% of men.

CHAPTER 4

Lifestyle Changes and Other Treatments

One of the more common beliefs about cardiovascular disease is that it is opportunistic—that it quietly lurks, waiting to strike people at random. Therefore, when the disease zeroes in on a particular individual, it is impossible for him or her to avoid its ill effects. However, medical experts say that notion is only another of the many myths about heart disease floating around in the public consciousness. The reality, says the Mayo Clinic, is that most heart disease, including cardiovascular disease, is preventable:

> And keeping your heart healthy doesn't require a lot of time and effort. Small changes, such as standing up and moving more, can make a difference. The changes don't need to be negative. In fact, one of the most important keys to [maintaining good heart health] is learning to enjoy a full and active life.[41]

Developing Healthy Habits Early

Several of these relatively small changes in lifestyle not only help to prevent cardiovascular disease, but are also among the preferred treatments for it when it is detected early. Lifestyle changes are generally noninvasive, meaning that when people adopt them, no objects or substances (medical instruments, drugs, and so forth) "invade" the body. Lifestyle changes are also fairly easy to implement and safe. When deciding which treatment or treatments are best for a patient, a doctor naturally hopes these noninvasive changes, sometimes called cardiac rehabilitation, will be successful.

It is true that such simple, straightforward treatments are not always enough by themselves. If a person has a more advanced case of cardiovascular disease and is in imminent danger of having a heart attack, lifestyle changes must be supplemented by medication or, in the worst cases, surgery. Yet when someone goes to the doctor at the first sign of cardiovascular problems, the lifestyle changes are frequently the only treatment necessary.

It is clear, therefore, that whether one is looking to prevent cardiovascular disease, treat it, or keep it from recurring once

Teens engage in cross-country running in California. Starting healthy exercise habits early significantly increases chances of living healthy throughout life.

it has been treated, these alterations in everyday behavior are essential to good heart health. Moreover, medical experts agree that adopting this healthy lifestyle is not a goal merely for elderly or even middle-aged folk. Rather, people of all ages, even teenagers and twenty-somethings, should do it. There is a tendency for those younger people to think they are invincible and that having some bad habits when young is no problem. After all, the common reasoning goes, a person can always become more careful and health-conscious later in life.

This approach, however, has always proven unwise. With rare exceptions, teenagers who have poor dietary habits, become overweight, smoke, fail to exercise regularly, and so forth tend to hold onto these behaviors for decades and sometimes for life. Those behaviors become habits that frequently are extremely difficult to break. Later, therefore, many of those once-carefree youngsters steadily develop a range of medical problems, including cardiovascular disease. The American Heart Association, American Medical Association, Centers for Disease Control and Prevention (CDC), Mayo Clinic, and numerous other leading medical groups all agree that it is far smarter to develop good personal habits when young and stick with them all through life.

Avoiding or Quitting Smoking

One behavior that heart patients should stop immediately and that younger people should avoid doing in the first place is smoking. Without a doubt, smoking is one of the biggest risk factors and causes of cardiovascular disease. Not only should smokers quit, they should also do their best to avoid contact with secondhand smoke. There is no doubt that doing so will be worth it in the long run. No matter how much or how long a person has smoked, immediately after quitting his or her risk of heart disease and stroke begins

dropping. In only a year or two, that individual's risk of developing heart disease decreases by half!

Granted, as everyone knows, quitting can be hard, particularly for heavy smokers and people who have smoked for many years. But help is available. Support groups composed of former smokers exist all across the United States and in many foreign countries. Also, all of the organizations mentioned above offer advice and in some cases step-by-step programs for quitting. The American Heart Association, for example, recommends this approach:

Think about quitting in 5 steps:

1. Set a Quit Date. Choose a date within the next seven days when you will quit smoking. Tell your family members and friends who are most likely to support your efforts.

2. Choose a method for quitting. There are three ways to quit smoking.

A student smokes outside a Colorado high school. Starting smoking from a young age is a leading cause of cardiovascular disease.

- Stop smoking all at once on your Quit Day.
- Reduce the number of cigarettes per day until you stop smoking completely.
- Smoke only part of your cigarette. If you use this method, you need to count how many puffs you take from each cigarette and reduce the number every 2 to 3 days.

3. Decide if you need medicines or other help to quit. Talk to your healthcare provider to discuss which medicine is best for you, and to get instructions about how to use it. These may include nicotine replacements (gum, spray, patch or inhaler) or prescription medicines such as bupropion hydrochloride or varenicline. You may also ask about referral to a smoking cessation program.
4. Plan for your Quit Day. Get rid of all cigarettes, matches, lighters, ashtrays from your house. Find healthy substitutes for smoking. Carry sugarless gum or mints. Munch carrots or celery sticks.
5. Stop smoking on your Quit Day.[42]

Routine Physical Activity

Quitting smoking is only a single step toward a heart-healthy lifestyle. All doctors and other medical professionals agree that achieving and maintaining such a lifestyle is near to impossible without getting regular exercise. In fact, exercise reduces the effects of several of the common risk factors for cardiovascular disease. These include LDL (the "bad" cholesterol), diabetes, and high blood pressure. Exercise also helps to raise levels of HDL, the "good" cholesterol.

The problem is that some people enjoy exercise and some do not. Interestingly, those who say they hate exercising complain that it is too regimented and boring. Usually, these individuals mistakenly equate the word or concept of exercise with repetitive, potentially tedious activities such as sit-ups, pushups, treadmill walking, stair-climbing, or crunches.

The truth, however, is that when doctors recommend regular exercise they do not mean only regimented, repetitious movements like sit-ups. In fact, all sorts of physical activi-

Quitting Smoking Can Be Hard

Doctors understand that quitting smoking can be extremely difficult for many people. To encourage people who are trying to quit, the American Heart Association lists some benefits of quitting:

- Your senses of smell and taste come back.
- Your smoker's cough goes away.
- Your digestive system returns to normal. . . .
- You breathe much easier. . . .
- You're free from the mess, smell and burns in clothing.
- You'll live longer and have less chance of heart disease, stroke, lung disease and cancer.

The group also has the following advice for people who smoke again after quitting:

It's hard to stay a nonsmoker once you've had a cigarette, so do everything you can to avoid that "one" [cigarette]. The urge to smoke will pass. The first 2 to 5 minutes will be the toughest. If you do smoke after quitting:

- This doesn't mean you're a smoker again—do something now to get back on track.
- Don't punish or blame yourself—tell yourself you're still a nonsmoker.
- Think about why you smoked and decide what to do differently the next time.
- Sign a contract to stay a nonsmoker.

American Heart Association. "How Can I Quit Smoking?." www.heart.org/HEARTORG/GettingHealthy/How-Can-I-Quit-Smoking_UCM_309000_Article.jsp.

ties can be classified as exercise as long as they get the body moving, stretching, and burning calories. These activities do not have to be overly strenuous and can be, and actually *should* be, fulfilling. As the National Heart, Lung, and Blood Institute puts it, "You don't have to be a marathon runner to benefit from physical activity. Do activities that you enjoy, and make them part of your daily routine."[43]

Some people like going for walks or bike rides, for instance. They say it can be fun because they can vary their routes and distances, as well as their destinations. Also, walking or biking with one or more friends can turn exercise sessions into pleasant social activities. The group can end up at a beach or park and have a picnic, swim, or informal softball game. Alternatively, the destination can be a shopping mall where the person or group goes shopping or takes in a movie.

High school teens hike in Asheville, North Carolina. Physical activity to improve cardiovascular health does not have to involve intense workouts.

In addition, all sorts of everyday activities can count as exercise. Often the trick is to avoid using conveniences such as elevators and escalators and take the stairs instead. Similarly, rather than send an email to a coworker in an office at the far end of the hall, get up and walk down to that office. Or instead of using a leaf blower, use an old-fashioned rake for a while. The main goal should be to frequently take advantage of opportunities that keep the body moving and to avoid sitting around for long periods of time. In addition, the American Heart Association adds some general tips to help ensure that this approach to healthy living will be successful:

> Do a variety of activities [and] make physical activity a routine so it becomes a habit. . . . If you stop for

any length of time, don't lose hope! Just get started again—slowly and work up to your old pace. . . . Try not to compare yourself with others. Your goal should be personal health and fitness. Think about whether you like to exercise alone or with other people, outside or inside, what time of day is best, and what kind of exercise you most enjoy doing. If you feel like quitting, remind yourself of all the reasons you started. Also think about how far you've come![44]

Stress Management and Support Groups

Another important aspect of treating heart disease through lifestyle changes is managing stress. An easy way to view stress is as the body's immediate response to change, particularly unwanted change. That reaction consists of increases in heart rate and breathing rate and a rise in blood pressure. A certain amount of stress as a response to change is normal and to be expected, but when stress becomes chronic, or constant, it can cause problems. It can make a person feel fearful, angry, overexcited, or vulnerable and powerless. Stress can also cause headaches and make it difficult to fall asleep. Moreover, when undergoing a lot of stress, a person is more likely to develop bad habits, including drinking too much alcohol, smoking, drug abuse, and overeating. In addition, chronic stress causes an increased risk for developing cardiovascular disease. Thus, to maintain a heart-healthy lifestyle, either to treat or to prevent heart disease, it is essential to manage one's stress levels.

Medical authorities suggest a number of ways to relieve stress on a regular basis. One is reaching out to relatives or friends and sharing personal feelings and concerns with them. Also, vigorous exercise or other physical activity has been proven to lessen stressful feelings. In addition, many doctors recommend trying to stay positive by transforming negative thoughts into more upbeat and optimistic ones. Still another approach is to take a fifteen-minute "breather" from life's routines once or twice a day by sitting quietly by oneself, relaxing, and taking long, even, restful breaths.

Dr. Sarah Samaan offers the following advice on how an often over-stressed group—stay-at-home moms—can reduce stress. Several major studies, she points out, show that:

Stay-at-home moms who spend more than twenty hours a week caring for their kids have a higher risk of heart disease than do women with no child-care responsibilities. Grandmothers who spend at least nine hours a week with their grandkids also carry a higher

A woman participates in a support group for military spouses at Camp Pendleton, California. Such groups can help with the stress of raising children while a spouse is deployed.

risk of heart attacks. So far, there are no good cardiac studies examining the interactions between work and child-rearing duties in men. If you're a woman, accept that raising children is stressful, no matter how much joy the sweet things bring. Children are your most vital responsibility. Nurture them and guide them, but don't neglect yourself. It's important to allow yourself time out to be your own person. If you have a partner or spouse, make sure that he or she is carrying a fair share of the load. If you're feeling overwhelmed, check in with your friends or relatives to see if you can help each other by sharing childcare responsibilities. If the burden feels too great, talk it over with your doctor and be sure that you are not suffering from depression.[45]

Some people undergoing treatment for cardiovascular disease do well with managing stress, but not so well with other aspects of maintaining a healthy lifestyle. In such cases, the doctor may feel that the patient's rehabilitation program needs an extra boost. He or she may therefore recommend attending a support group. Such a group will consist of several other people who have cardiovascular disease and are undergoing some form of treatment. Each person in the group talks about his or her own experiences. This shows the other members they are not alone and that their situation is neither unusual nor hopeless. Also, a member may offer tips to the others on how he or she successfully handled a stressful situation. Such groups typically meet in community centers, hospitals, YMCAs, and so forth.

Heart Medications

Although these and other lifestyle changes are widely prescribed by doctors to help heart disease patients, more advanced cases of cardiovascular disease often require more forceful treatments. The least invasive of these is prescribing medication. Certain drugs can make the heart work less hard, decrease blood pressure and LDL cholesterol levels, prevent the formation of blood clots, and in some cases delay the need for surgery.

Aspirin: To Take or Not to Take

Television commercials frequently mention using aspirin to prevent heart attacks. The American Medical Association here presents the actual facts surrounding this claim, including who can and who should not take aspirin.

A person with diabetes tends to form blood clots more easily than most people, and aspirin appears to keep red blood cells from forming clots. Your doctor can recommend the lowest possible dosage for you, usually between 81 and 162 milligrams. Because some people experience irritation of the stomach lining from taking aspirin, you may prefer to take enteric-coated aspirin tablets. The coating enables the aspirin to pass through your stomach without dissolving. It dissolves in your intestine instead, reducing the risk of unpleasant side effects such as stomach pain or nausea. Some people cannot safely take aspirin every day. You should not take it if you know you are allergic to it; you have a tendency to bleed easily; you have had bleeding from your digestive tract recently; you have liver disease; or you are under twenty-one years old (as the effects of aspirin on younger people have not been fully studied).

Martin S. Lipsky et al. *American Medical Association Guide to Preventing and Treating Heart Disease.* New York: Wiley and Sons, 2008, p. 109.

One common kind of medicine used to treat adverse cardiovascular symptoms is called an anticoagulant. By thinning the blood a bit, this type of drug makes the formation of dangerous clots less likely. Aspirin is another substance with anti-clotting properties. Other frequently prescribed heart medicines include ACE inhibitors, which are drugs that widen blood vessels and thereby lower blood pressure;

beta blockers that lower blood pressure by decreasing heart rate; and calcium channel blockers, which increase blood supply and oxygen to the heart.

Medical authorities say they cannot overstate how important it is that heart patients do not try to choose and take such medications on their own. Those that do make this mistake often search for articles about those drugs online. But as Marc Gillinov and Steven Nissen point out:

> One source of information should always be avoided: websites produced by the drug makers. These sites abound. In fact, if you type the brand name of a drug into a search engine, you will usually find a website administered by the drug manufacturer at the top of the list. Such websites are designed to promote use of the drug and are unreliable sources of information. [Instead] get information from your doctor.[46]

Angioplasty and Surgery

In more serious cases of cardiovascular disease, a doctor may have to resort to still more invasive techniques. Surgery is a technique in which a doctor uses a sharp instrument, such as a scalpel, to cut into the body. There is a procedure for treating heart disease called angioplasty that decidedly does invade the body, but does so without resorting to surgery. In this procedure, a doctor unblocks one or more arteries that have been narrowed or completely obstructed by plaque. He or she takes a thin, flexible tube with a balloon attached to the front end and injects it into a strategically chosen blood vessel. Carefully and steadily, the tube is threaded through the body until it reaches the blocked artery. Then the physician sends air through the tube, inflating the balloon, which in turn pushes the plaque against the artery's walls. Blood flow is thereby restored. At that point, depending on the circumstances, the doctor may or may not decide to insert a tiny artificial tube called a stent into the affected artery. The stent supports the vessel's walls and helps to prevent later blockages.

In some cases, for instance when a blocked artery lies in a spot too difficult for the balloon and stent to reach safely,

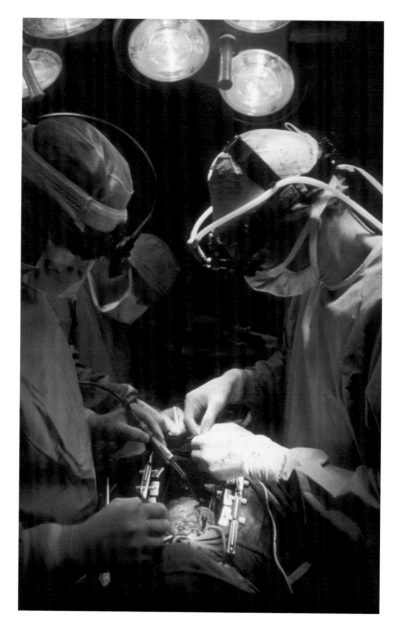

angioplasty is not a good option. When that happens, the doctor may turn to open-heart surgery. The most common variety in the United States, the heart bypass, improves blood flow to the heart when one or more arteries are blocked. During the operation, the surgeon takes a healthy artery or vein from an arm, leg, or somewhere else in the body. He or she then connects one end to a spot just before the blockage in an artery and the other end to a spot just beyond the blockage. In this way, the healthy vessel bypasses, or goes around, the blocked section, providing a new route for blood to take to the heart.

In a few cases, the heart has been so damaged by cardiovascular disease that doctors are sure the organ will not last much longer. The patient thereby becomes a candidate for a heart transplant. In this very complex and risky surgery, the patient's dying heart is removed and replaced with a healthy heart from a deceased donor. Not surprisingly, the number of people who donate their hearts this way in their wills is small, so donated hearts are in extremely short supply. As a result, medical facilities employ a rigorous selection process in choosing the patients who will receive those hearts. On the one hand, such a person must be sick enough to badly need a new heart, while on the other he or she must be strong enough that the shock of the operation will not be fatal.

As the surgery begins, the surgeon opens the patient's chest and hooks up the lungs and major arteries to a device called a heart-lung machine. It keeps the patient's blood pumping through the body while the old heart is removed and the new one inserted in its place. From start to finish, this kind of surgery takes many hours and involves a large team of medical professionals.

In the initial years of heart transplants, in the late 1960s and into the 1970s, survival rates for transplant patients were low. But they have markedly improved over the years. In the early 2010s, close to 90 percent of transplant patients can expect to live for at least a year after the surgery. Roughly 75 percent will survive for five years, and a bit more than half will likely live for ten years or more.

Daring Experiments and Advances

These constantly improving survival rates of heart transplant patients attest to how far the various treatments for cardiovascular disease have come in only a few decades. This tremendous progress is in part a tribute to the talent and dedication of thousands of doctors, surgeons, and other medical professionals both in the United States and around the world.

In equal measure, those rapid improvements are the result of phenomenal advances in medical science and technology. It is important to emphasize that such progress has by no means reached its peak, but it continues at full speed. "We foresee tremendous advances over the next few decades," two leading heart doctors state.[47]

One area in which researchers have sunk a great deal of money, time, and effort is the goal of creating reliable artificial hearts. Because only a select few patients end up with new hearts via transplantation, each year thousands of people who badly need new hearts do not get them and die as a result. A human-made heart that functions like the real thing would extend the lives of most of those people.

An artificial heart produced by biomedical firm Carmat is shown at a hospital in Paris, France, in 2013.

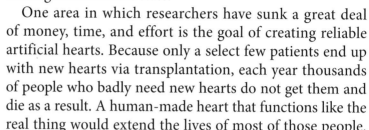

So far, a few artificial hearts have been constructed and implanted, but the survival rates have been very low. Yet according to Gillinov and Nissen, these failures are merely the prelude to a far brighter future:

> Researchers are busily working to develop the next generation of artificial hearts. The goal is to produce a small, fully implantable device that will last five years or longer. It will not suffer from mechanical failure and will not cause blood clots that can lead to strokes. Devices with these features have already been implanted in animals, and early results look promising. Our prediction: Unlike the search for the holy grail, the quest for a reliable total artificial heart will occur over decades, rather than centuries, and will come to a successful conclusion.[48]

Another area in which experts foresee major advances in treating heart disease is stem cells. These are cells that the body has not yet told to become specific types—such as liver cells, brain cells, or skin cells. The goal is to teach a mass of stem cells to grow into whatever kind of tissue is needed. For example, some researchers are trying to make stem cells turn into healthy skin cells in hopes of replacing the damaged skin of burn victims.

Similarly, other researchers are attempting to coax stem cells into becoming healthy heart tissue. That tissue might someday be used to replace damaged tissue in the heart's walls. Even if that goal is not possible, some cardiac specialists say, the stem cells introduced to the heart may still be extremely beneficial. They may secrete chemicals that will stimulate blood vessel growth or even cause the damaged heart cells to generate new, healthy ones.

Reliable artificial hearts and the use of stem cells to repair damaged hearts represent only the tip of the proverbial iceberg of advanced heart treatment research. Other scientists are studying ways to use a map of a child's genes to determine if he or she will later have a high risk of heart disease. If the child does show that tendency, he or she would be given a specialized medical plan to follow that would greatly reduce the chances of developing cardiovascular disease. Still other researchers are working on ways to use magnets to move beneficial cells to the heart area and keep them there permanently. In light of such daring experiments and advances, Samaan remarks:

> We are fortunate to live in a time of tremendous progress in medical science. As I write, new developments and discoveries are emerging, and I have no doubt that our understanding of heart disease . . . will continue to evolve. It is an exciting time to be a cardiologist.[49]

CHAPTER 5

A Heart-Healthy Diet for Life

It has been established that starting a regular exercise plan, quitting smoking, lowering one's blood pressure, reducing stress, angioplasty, and various kinds of surgery are among the many forms of treatment for cardiovascular disease. There is one more extremely important one that all cardiovascular patients should adopt. That includes those who do not need surgery and those who have had surgery and survived it. In fact, doctors even recommend this lifestyle habit for people who have never had any cardiovascular problems at all, since it will likely help them to avoid ever developing such problems. It is therefore a preventative as well as a treatment for cardiovascular disease.

The habit in question, which so neatly combines treatment and prevention, is eating a heart-healthy diet not only on a daily basis, but for life. There is an old adage that says, "You are what you eat." Few old sayings are as truthful as this one is, for people with chronic poor diets, including children and teenagers, invariably develop all sorts of physical ailments over time. These range from diabetes, vitamin deficiencies, and digestive problems to high blood pressure, obesity, and cholesterol-clogged arteries, to name only a few. Moreover, several of these problems are clearly major risk factors for cardiovascular disease. Conversely, numerous

A breakfast of oatmeal and fresh fruit is one way to start a heart-healthy day

studies have shown that people who regularly consume a healthy diet are much less likely to develop most of these problems.

What Weight Is Best?

Of the ailments listed above, it is instructive to briefly single out obesity. Not only is being seriously overweight a direct result of poor eating habits, it also increases the severity of nearly all the other physical problems mentioned. That includes cardiovascular disease. Thus, adopting a heart-healthy diet is especially important for people who are

ADULT BODY MASS INDEX (BMI) CHART

BMI	Healthy Weight						Overweight					Obese					
	19	20	21	22	23	24	25	26	27	28	29	30	31	32	33	34	35
Height	Weight (in pounds)																
4'10"	91	96	100	105	110	115	119	124	129	134	138	143	148	153	158	162	167
4'11"	94	99	104	109	114	119	124	128	133	138	143	148	153	158	163	168	173
5'0"	97	102	107	112	118	123	128	133	138	143	148	153	158	163	168	174	179
5'1"	100	106	111	116	122	127	132	137	143	148	153	158	164	169	174	180	185
5'2"	104	109	115	120	126	131	136	142	147	153	158	164	169	175	180	186	191
5'3"	107	113	118	124	130	135	141	146	152	158	163	169	175	180	186	191	197
5'4"	110	116	122	128	134	140	145	151	157	163	169	174	180	186	192	197	204
5'5"	114	120	126	132	138	144	150	156	162	168	174	180	186	192	198	204	210
5'6"	118	124	130	136	142	148	155	161	167	173	179	186	192	198	204	210	216
5'7"	121	127	134	140	146	153	159	166	172	178	185	191	198	204	211	217	223
5'8"	125	131	138	144	151	158	164	171	177	184	190	197	203	210	216	223	230
5'9"	128	135	142	149	155	162	169	176	182	189	196	203	209	216	223	230	236
5'10"	132	139	146	153	160	167	174	181	188	195	202	209	216	222	229	236	243
5'11"	136	143	150	157	165	172	179	186	193	200	208	215	222	229	236	243	250
6'0"	140	147	154	162	169	177	184	191	199	206	213	221	228	235	242	250	258
6'1"	144	151	159	166	174	182	189	197	204	212	219	227	235	242	250	257	265
6'2"	148	155	163	171	179	186	194	202	210	218	225	233	241	249	256	264	272
6'3"	152	160	168	176	184	192	200	208	216	224	232	240	248	256	264	272	279
6'4"	156	164	172	180	189	197	205	213	221	230	238	246	254	263	271	279	287

Note: For adults 20 years old and older, BMI is calculated using the same categories for all ages and for both men and women, as shown above. For ages 2 through 19, BMI is calculated as a for-age percentile and varies by age and by sex.

Source: National Heart, Blood and Lung Institute. "Body Mass Index Table 1." National Institutes of Health. www.nhlbi.nih.gov/guidelines/obesity/bmi_tbl.htm.

more than a few pounds overweight. Plainly, such a person should aim for reaching and staying at the weight that is most healthy for him or her. But how does one determine what weight is best?

The answer given by a majority of physicians and medical clinics is to try to maintain one's ideal body mass index. Abbreviated BMI, it is a measure of body fat calculated using weight and height. An easy way to understand it is to visualize a human body's frame—that is, its bones and muscles. In general, the taller a person is, the longer and thicker his or her frame is, and therefore the more that individual can safely weigh. The National Heart, Lung, and Blood Institute provides a handy BMI calculator on their website at www.nhlbi.

Obesity rates continue to increase around the world. A BMI calculator can be used to establish what weight range is healthy for your height.

nih.gov/guidelines/obesity/BMI/bmi-calc.htm. Other major health organizations and clinics offer similar versions.

Entering one's weight and height into the calculator produces a number representing that person's BMI. If it is between 25 and 29.9, he or she is considered overweight, and the person is considered obese if the number is 30 or more. The ideal number is somewhere in the range of 19 to 25. For example, a person who is 5 foot 6 inches tall and weighs 150 pounds has a BMI of 24.2, which doctors view as very healthy. Someone the same height who weighs 135 pounds has a BMI of 21.8, which is also considered healthy. Keep in mind that these figures are general and will vary somewhat from person to person.

If one is obese, it is best to consult with a doctor or licensed nutritionist for guidance in the best course for losing weight. But one sound piece of advice for anyone who is overweight, no matter how much, is to avoid fad diets. These are widely advertised "reducing" or "eat less" diets designed primarily to shed pounds. The problem is that in the vast majority of cases, the dieter abandons the diet when he or she reaches the goal weight and returns to his or her former eating habits. Over time, the person gains most or all of the weight back.

In contrast, doctors say, it is better not to define the word *diet* as a plan for losing weight. Instead, one should embrace its other definition—the sum of the various foods that a person eats on a daily basis. The aim, therefore, should be to adopt an "eat right" or "eat healthy" diet that one can and will stay on for life. Combined with regular exercise, such a healthy eating plan will stimulate an overweight person's body to slowly but steadily return to the proper BMI.

Diets Around the Globe

Partly because of the glut of diet books in libraries and bookstores, along with food and exercise programs on television, most people find it difficult to determine which diet is the healthiest. Here is where the U.S., European,

NUTRITION FACT
30,000–100,000
Deaths from cardiovascular disease each year in the United States caused by eating foods high in trans fats.

A shopper in the Central Market in Athens, Greece, purchases fresh fruits and vegetables, part of what scientists call the heart-healthy Mediterranean diet.

and global medical establishments can offer solid, useful guidance. Over the past few decades, several major scientific studies examined average diets in various parts of the world. Perhaps the most famous was the landmark Seven Countries Study, which began in the late 1950s. It looked in great detail at the diets of twelve different local populations in five European nations, Japan, and the United States. The investigators tracked the eating habits and changing health patterns of more than 12,700 men for several decades, yielding a treasure trove of information about the effects of diet on human health.

Among the results is that the average diet in the United States and northern Europe, often called the Western diet, is the least healthy and most damaging. It has been found that people in those countries tend to consume a lot of red meat, pastries and other foods containing a lot of highly processed sugar and flour, large amounts of unhealthy fats, and too much salt. As a result, the rates of cardiovascular disease and death by heart attack and stroke in those countries is disturbingly high.

By contrast, Greece and most other countries bordering the Mediterranean Sea have around one-fifth as many cases of cardiovascular disease and heart-related mortality. Regardless of rates of smoking, exercise, and other risk factors for heart disease in those nations, their average residents are far freer of heart problems and healthier in general than Americans and northern Europeans. Those findings have been verified by another later large-scale study of the diets of Mediterranean people that ended in 2008. In the words of Dr. Anthony Komaroff, a professor at Harvard Medical School, "Beginning in 2003, researchers recruited nearly 7,500 Spaniards to take part in the [study]. All participants were over age 55, and none had been diagnosed with heart disease—though all were at high risk for developing it." The study "stopped early, after just under five years of follow-up, when the independent board charged with an ongoing review of the results determined that there had been significantly fewer heart attacks, strokes, and deaths from cardiovascular disease in the Mediterranean groups."[50]

Meats, Fruits, Vegetables, and Grains

Thanks to what doctors have learned from these and several similar studies, the so-called Mediterranean diet has emerged as the single most highly recommended diet by medical experts in many countries, including the United States. An examination of the most common foods and drinks it entails reveals why it is so healthy. First, it mostly

Reducing Salt Intake

In addition to recommending the consumption of plenty of fruits, vegetables, and whole grains, the DASH (Dietary Approaches to Stop Hypertension) diet strongly emphasizes reducing salt intake. (Because salt is mostly sodium, the terms *salt* and *sodium* are often used interchangeably.) A Harvard Medical School publication advises:

> Processed foods and prepared foods are the greatest sources of sodium in the American diet (75 percent by some estimates). By choosing fresh foods, you can decide how much or how little salt to add. Processed, cured meats typically have much more sodium than fresh meats, and canned vegetables usually have more sodium than fresh vegetables. . . . For many foods and preparations, the average person can't detect moderate to substantial differences in sodium levels, including reductions of up to as much as 25 percent. That's great news. In fact, many food manufacturers and restaurant companies have already made or are in the process of making substantial cuts in sodium. [Moreover] studies have found that we can shift our sense of taste to enjoy foods with lower levels of sodium. One key to success: Make the changes gradually and . . . as time goes on, you won't miss the salt.

Harvard Medical School. "Strategies for Cutting Back on Salt." www.health .harvard.edu/newsletters/Harvard_Heart_Letter/2010/July/strategies-for-cutting -back-on-salt.

eliminates red meat, which has high levels of cholesterol and saturated fats. Also, a 2013 study found that red meat contains large amounts of a microscopic material called L-carnitine. When it reaches the intestines, some of the bacteria there transform it into a substance that contributes to hardening of the arteries.

In contrast, the Mediterranean diet mostly replaces beef and other red meats with fish and small amounts of chicken, turkey, or other poultry. These flesh foods contain significantly less cholesterol than red meat. Furthermore, although they do contain L-carnitine, they have far less of it per pound than red meat does. The substitution of fish and poultry for red meat alone significantly lowers risk factors for cardiovascular disease.

Second, people who live on the Mediterranean diet eat several servings of fruits and vegetables every day. They also consume bread and other foods made from either unprocessed or minimally processed whole grains several times per week. These foods are high in complex carbohydrates. Carbohydrates, or carbs for short, are substances that produce energy required by the body's cells, tissues, and organs. The three main kinds of carbohydrates are sugars, starches, and fibers. Complex carbohydrates are versions that are healthy in large part because they have not been processed, or refined, and thereby stripped of most of their fiber and nutrients.

The stripped versions are called simple carbohydrates. They are found in white bread and pasta made from

Whole-grain breads contain high amounts of fiber and complex carbohydrates that can make one feel fuller longer.

processed flour; doughnuts, cake, pastries, and other goodies made from processed flour and refined sugar and high in fat; and colas and other sodas, among many other widely popular foods. Because of their lack of nutrients and fiber, simple carbs quickly break down into simple sugars in the digestive tract and promote weight gain, diabetes, and cardiovascular disease.

Clearly, the high amounts of fiber in complex carbohydrates are one important reason why foods containing these carbs are healthy. Dr. Sarah Samaan explains:

> Soluble fiber from sources such oat bran, apples, oranges, prunes, and legumes (beans) can help lower your cholesterol, mainly by decreasing the absorption of cholesterol through the gastrointestinal tract [the stomach and intestines]. The insoluble form of fiber that comes from seeds, whole grains, and brown rice does not have the same cholesterol-lowering effect, but has other benefits. . . . Fiber helps maintain good digestive health [and] a diet with plenty of fiber will make you feel fuller faster. My patient Jessica credits her before-meal apples for her 20-pound weight loss this year.[51]

Dairy Products and Olive Oil

The Mediterranean diet also features several servings per week of foods such as nuts, seeds, tomatoes, garlic, and onions, all of which have been proven to be extremely healthy for the body. In addition, the diet includes cheese, yogurt, and a few other dairy products. However, these are mostly low in fat and eaten in moderate quantities. According to Oldways, a nonprofit organization that teaches good nutrition:

> Cheese and yogurt are eaten regularly in the traditional Mediterranean diet, but in low to moderate amounts. The calcium in cheese and yogurt is important for bone and heart health. Low-fat and nonfat dairy products

ease concerns of adverse consequences of somewhat higher consumption of dairy products. Dairy products common to the traditional Mediterranean diet include: brie, chevre, corvo, feta, haloumi, manchego, Parmigiano-Reggiano, pecorino, ricotta, and yogurt (including Greek yogurt).[52]

Still another heart-healthy benefit of the Mediterranean diet is the use of olive oil rather than butter, margarine, or oils high in fat, which are widely consumed in the Western diet. In Greece and other lands bordering the Mediterranean, olive oil is the main cooking medium and is also employed in baking and creating salad dressings and various sauces. Olive oil does contain fat, but it is mostly health-promoting rather than unhealthy. About 75 percent of the fat is composed of oleic acid, which has been shown to significantly reduce the amount of LDL ("bad cholesterol") in a person's blood.

Olive oil's healthy fat also appears to help lower high

Olive oil has been shown to have many health benefits and is used extensively throughout the Mediterranean area.

Olive Oil's "Magical Properties"

As cardiologists Marc Gillinov and Steven Nissen point out in their book about heart disease, much of the attention given in recent years to the Mediterranean diet "centers on the 'magical' properties of olive oil." They examine the background and possible benefits of the substance:

> The ancient Greeks and Romans believed that olive oil conferred strength and youth, and it was used to produce both medicines and cosmetics. The Romans planted olive trees along the entire Mediterranean, profiting from commerce in this special commodity. Today, that commerce continues, and 99 percent of the world's olive oil is produced by countries bordering the Mediterranean Sea. . . . We now recognize that olive oil contains a wide variety of substances that can affect cardiovascular health. These range from its monounsaturated fatty acids [fats that are healthy for the body], to components that reduce inflammation [swelling] and may act as antioxidants [substances thought to protect the body's cells]. For scientists, olive oil remains an object of fascination, as we work to improve our understanding of the mechanisms by which it may influence the heart. For the rest of us, olive oil offers a combination of good taste and good health.

Marc Gillinov and Steven Nissen. *Heart 411: The Only Guide to Heart Health You'll Ever Need.* New York: Three Rivers, 2012, p. 95.

blood pressure. Still another health benefit of olive oil is that it has supplies of antioxidants, including vitamin E and beta-carotene. Some experts think these substances delay or prevent cell damage caused by aging and other factors. All of these advantages make olive oil an almost ideal food for discouraging the development of cardiovascular disease.

Red Wine

Olive oil is not the only liquid substance included in the Mediterranean diet, as red wine is consumed regularly in the Mediterranean countries. Wine contains alcohol, and it is well known that consumption of too much alcohol is detrimental to health. It can be addictive and it can damage various vital organs, including the liver and heart. It is only natural, therefore, to ask why and how drinking red wine almost every day can be healthy.

The answer to that question is twofold. First, the vast majority of people in Greece and other Mediterranean countries who drink wine as part of their traditional diet do so in moderation. In this case, "in moderation" translates to no more than one five-ounce glass each day for women and no more than two five-ounce glasses for men.

When consumed in moderation, wine has been shown to protect against some aspects of cardiovascular disease.

Second, when consumed in small amounts like that, red wine (and white wine, too) actually has two known effects on the body that protect against heart attacks and some other aspects of cardiovascular disease. One is the stimulation of beneficial changes in cholesterol levels, as explained by cardiologists Marc Gillinov and Steven Nissen:

> Your levels of the different types of cholesterol help determine your risk of heart disease. Alcohol affects both LDL and HDL cholesterol levels. Laboratory studies demonstrate that alcohol blocks the oxidation of [addition of oxygen molecules to] LDL, which is favorable, because oxidation of LDL leads to the formation of fatty plaques in the arteries of the heart. However, the effect of alcohol on HDL is likely more important. Moderate alcohol consumption increases HDL by about 12 percent, which in turn may reduce the risk of developing heart disease. Proponents claim that 50 percent of alcohol's heart benefit can be attributed to this change in HDL cholesterol levels. By way of comparison, this extent of increase in "good" cholesterol is similar to the effects of an aerobic exercise program.[53]

The other physical benefit of alcohol is its effect on blood clotting. It is the formation of a blood clot at the site of accumulated plaque in an artery, of course, that can trigger a heart attack. Simply put, certain properties of small amounts of alcohol slightly thin the blood, which makes clot formation a bit more difficult. Also, one key substance in the clot formation process is a protein called fibrinogen. As it happens, a small quantity of alcohol in the blood each day somewhat decreases fibrinogen levels. In turn, that, too, makes it harder for blood to clot and by extension makes the onset of a heart attack less likely.

The jury is still out on whether Americans and other Westerners will fully adopt the Mediterranean diet, including its wine-drinking component, in the years to come. In that regard, it is crucial to point out that the wine drinking is not by any means essential to that eating plan. Doctors point out that the other components of the diet are heart-healthy in and of themselves, so the wine part of the diet can be safely eliminated if one prefers.

"It's Not Rocket Science!"

Although the Mediterranean diet is highly recommended by doctors across the United States, they and many other experts also advocate another heart-healthy approach to lifetime eating. It is called the DASH diet. (The letters stand for Dietary Approaches to Stop Hypertension. Hypertension is another name for chronic high blood pressure.) It was developed in the 1990s by the National Heart, Lung, and Blood Institute, which conducted a major study of heart-healthy eating. Aiding in the study were five well-respected American medical research facilities—those at Brigham and Women's Hospital in Boston, Massachusetts; Johns Hopkins University in Baltimore, Maryland; Pennington Biomedical Research Center in Baton Rouge, Louisiana; Duke University in Durham, North Carolina; and Kaiser Permanente Center for Health Research in Portland, Oregon.

A market stall in Laos offers fresh fish and vegetables, two heart-healthy foods that may prevent cardiovascular disease.

The DASH diet consists of eating lots of fruits and vegetables, along with some low-fat dairy foods. It also discourages eating red meat and suggests replacing it with fish or chicken and other kinds of poultry. Nuts and foods made from whole grains are also highly recommended, as is reducing one's intake of sweets and other fatty foods and lowering one's salt intake. Sound familiar? It should, because with the exception of recommending the use of olive oil and a daily glass of wine, the DASH diet is extremely similar to the Mediterranean diet.

This only serves to show that close to every major modern medical study of human diet has come to roughly the same conclusions about which foods are the most heart-healthy. Also, the fact that medical science has largely determined the healthiest diet is a boon to the average person. Whether he or she has or has not yet developed cardiovascular disease, knowing the best foods to eat day after day and year after year is a hugely valuable tool. One of the best things about this knowledge that virtually anyone, anywhere can apply it to his or her own life with the assurance that it will be beneficial.

Moreover, with a little motivation and self-discipline, anyone—male or female, young or old, rich or poor—can learn to combine healthy eating with regular exercise and other heart-healthy behaviors. As another useful old saying puts it, "It's not rocket science!" Any and all of us now have the means of making cardiovascular disease and heart attacks as rare as they once were. As the Mayo Clinic phrases it:

> The good news is that most heart disease is preventable. Many risk factors for heart disease are factors you can change. If an emergency happens, prompt action can save your life. If you already have a heart condition, there's a lot you can do to make sure you live well despite your condition. The take-away message: You have far more control over your heart health than you may realize.[54]

Introduction: Myths About Cardiovascular Disease

1. Sarah Samaan. *Best Practices for a Healthy Heart: How to Stop Heart Disease Before or After It Starts.* New York: The Experiment, 2011, p. xiii.
2. American Heart Association. "Top 10 Myths About Cardiovascular Disease." www.heart.org/HEART ORG/Conditions/Top-10-Myths -about-Cardiovascular-Disease _UCM_430164_Article.jsp.
3. Samaan, *Best Practices for a Healthy Heart*, pp. 5–6.
4. Mayo Clinic. *Healthy Heart for Life!* New York: Time Home Entertainment, 2012, p. 12.
5. Jennifer H. Mieres. "Your Heart's Health Is In Your Hands." In American Heart Association. *Complete Guide to Women's Heart Health: The Go Red for Women Way to Well-Being and Vitality.* New York: Clarkson Potter, pp. 4, 6.

Chapter 1: The Number-One Killer

6. Marc Gillinov and Steven Nissen. *Heart 411: The Only Guide to Heart Health You'll Ever Need.* New York: Three Rivers Press, 2012, p. 449.
7. Samaan, *Best Practices for a Healthy Heart*, p. 3.
8. Martin S. Lipsky et al. *American Medical Association Guide to Preventing and Treating Heart Disease.* New York: Wiley and Sons, 2008, p. 19.
9. Attah-Effah Badu. "55 Million People Died Worldwide in 2011—WHO." *Daily Express*, August 6, 2013. http://dailyexpressonline.com /55-million-people-died-worldwide -in-2011-who-2013-08-06.
10. Franklin Institute. "History of the Heart." www.fi.edu/learn/heart/hi story/history.html.
11. Helen Valborg. *Symbols of the Eternal Doctrine.* Washington, D.C.: Theosophy Trust, 2007, pp. 112–113.
12. Quoted in Paula Findlen and Stanford University Department of History. "A History of the Heart." www.stanford.edu/class/history13 /earlysciencelab/body/heartpages /heart.html.
13. Quoted in Findlen and Stanford University Department of History. "A History of the Heart."
14. Sujata K. Bhatia, *Biomaterials for Clinical Applications.* New York: Springer, 2010, p. 23.

15. Quoted in Lawrence Deckelbaum. "Heart Attacks and Coronary Artery Disease." In Barry L. Zaret et al. *Yale University School of Medicine Heart Book.* New York: William Morrow, 2002, p. 133.

16. Franklin Institute. "History of the Heart."

17. Gillinov and Nissen. *Heart 411,* p. 369.

Chapter 2: Major Causes and Complications

18. Dr. Ken Stein, Boston Scientific. "How Your Heart Works." www .bostonscientific.com/lifebeat -online/heart-smart/how-your -heart-works.html.

19. Lipsky. *American Medical Association Guide to Preventing and Treating Heart Disease,* p. 23.

20. Lipsky. *American Medical Association Guide to Preventing and Treating Heart Disease,* pp. 69–70.

21. British Heart Foundation. "Smoking." www.bhf.org.uk/heart-health /prevention/smoking.aspx.

22. Harvard Medical School. "Premature Heart Disease." www.health .harvard.edu/newsletters/Har vard_Mens_Health_Watch/2009 /November/premature-heart -disease.

23. Gillinov and Nissen. *Heart 411,* p. 452.

24. Lipsky. *American Medical Association Guide to Preventing and Treating Heart Disease,* p. 43.

25. "Statistics Related to Overweight and Obesity." Cleveland Clinic website, November 12, 2012. http://my .clevelandclinic.org/disorders /obesity/hic_statistics_related_to _overweight_and_obesity.aspx.

26. Mark Hyman. "How Eating at Home Can Save Your Life." www .huffingtonpost.com/dr-mark -hyman/family-dinner-how_b _806114.html.

27. Hyman. "How Eating at Home Can Save Your Life."

28. Samaan. *Best Practices for a Healthy Heart,* p. 14.

29. Lipsky. *American Medical Association Guide to Preventing and Treating Heart Disease,* p. 21.

30. Quoted in Mayo Clinic. *Healthy Heart for Life!,* p. 145.

31. Gillinov and Nissen. *Heart 411,* p. 385.

Chapter 3: Symptoms and Medical Diagnosis

32. Women's Health.gov. "An Interview with a Woman Living with Heart Disease." www.womenshealth.gov /news/spotlights/2014/2.html.

33. Women's Health.gov. "An Interview with a Woman Living with Heart Disease."

34. Women's Health.gov. "An Interview with a Woman Living with Heart Disease."

35. Mayo Clinic. "Heart Disease Symptoms." www.mayoclinic.org/diseas es-conditions/heart-disease/basics /symptoms/con-20034056.

36. Woman's Health.gov. "Heart Dis-

ease Fact Sheet." http://womens
health.gov/publications/our
-publications/fact-sheet/heart
-disease.html.

37. Texas Heart Institute. "Electrocardiogram." http://texasheartinstitute
.org/HIC/Topics/Diag/diekg.cfm.

38. Samaan. *Best Practices for a Healthy Heart*, pp. 9–10.

39. Medline Plus. "Coronary Angiography." www.nlm.nih.gov/medline
plus/ency/article/003876.htm.

40. Texas Heart Institute. "Cardiac Magnetic Resonance Imaging." http:
//texasheartinstitute.org/HIC
/Topics/Diag/dimri.cfm.

Chapter 4: Lifestyle Changes and Other Treatments

41. Mayo Clinic. *Healthy Heart for Life!*, p. 6.

42. American Heart Association. "How
Can I Quit Smoking?" www.heart
.org/HEARTORG/GettingHealthy
/How-Can-I-Quit-Smoking_UC
M_309000_Article.jsp.

43. National Heart, Lung, and Blood
Institute. "Getting Started and
Staying Active." www.nhlbi.nih
.gov/health/health-topics/topics
/phys/getstarted.html.

44. American Heart Association. "How
Can Physical Activity Become a
Way of Life?" www.heart.org/HE

ARTORG/GettingHealthy/How
-Can-Physical-Activity-Become-a
-Way-of-Life_UCM_308998_Ar
ticle.jsp.

45. Samaan. *Best Practices for a Healthy Heart*, p. 193.

46. Gillinov and Nissen. *Heart 411*, p. 261.

47. Gillinov and Nissen. *Heart 411*, p. 499.

48. Gillinov and Nissen. *Heart 411*, p. 505.

49. Samaan. *Best Practices for a Healthy Heart*, p. 344.

Chapter 5: A Heart-Healthy Diet for Life

50. Anthony Komaroff. "Study Supports Health Benefits from Mediterranean Style Diets." www.health
.harvard.edu/blog/study-supports
-heart-benefits-from-mediter
ranean-style-diets-201302255930.

51. Samaan. *Best Practices for a Healthy Heart*, p. 65.

52. Oldways. "Traditional Med Diet."
http://oldwayspt.org/resources
/heritage-pyramids/mediterranean
-diet-pyramid/traditional-med
-diet.

53. Gillinov and Nissen. *Heart 411*, pp. 127–128.

54. Mayo Clinic. *Healthy Heart for Life!*, p. 9.

aneurysm: An outward swelling in an artery's wall or the heart's tissue caused by the pressure of blood against a weakened area.

angina (full name is angina pectoris): Discomfort or pain in the chest caused by an insufficient flow of blood to the heart.

angiogram (or coronary angiography): A medical test in which a special dye injected into the blood is visible in an X-ray, thereby creating an image of the heart and surrounding blood vessels.

angioplasty: A surgical procedure in which a balloon-tipped tube is inserted into a clogged artery in order to unclog it.

aorta: The major artery that runs from the heart down into the abdomen, carrying oxygenated blood to the body.

atherosclerosis: "Hardening of the arteries"; the disease process in which the inner walls of various arteries become coated with plaque.

blood cholesterol: A waxy material that normally circulates through the bloodstream.

body mass index: A formula that compares a person's weight to his or her height to determine whether that person is overweight or obese.

bypass surgery: An operation in which a healthy piece of a blood vessel is connected to a blocked artery in such a way that it bypasses, or goes around, the blockage, restoring healthy blood flow.

carbohydrates: Food substances that produce energy used by the body's cells and tissues.

cardiac arrest: When the heart suddenly stops beating.

cardiac rehabilitation: Another name for a series of heart-healthy lifestyle changes, including exercising regularly, stopping smoking, and managing stress.

cardiologist: A physician who specializes in the heart and its diseases.

cardiovascular: Having to do with the heart and blood vessels.

cardiovascular disease: Also called coronary artery disease (CAD) and coronary heart disease (CHD); an illness characterized by several heart-related conditions, including high blood pressure, atherosclerosis, heart failure, and heart attack.

carnitine: A substance in meat and other flesh foods that, once inside the body, promotes hardening of the arteries.

chronic: Persistent or long-lasting.

depression: A medical condition characterized by prolonged, deep sadness.

diabetes: A disease in which sugars build up in the blood.

dietary cholesterol: A fatlike substance that exists in eggs, meat, dairy products, and some other foods.

edema: A swelling of the feet or hands caused by the body's retention of too many fluids.

fibrinogen: A protein that aids in the formation of blood clots.

HDL (high-density lipoprotein): Of the two main types of cholesterol, the "good cholesterol."

heart attack: Tissue damage to the heart muscle caused by a stoppage of oxygenated blood through one or more major arteries.

heart failure: A reduction in the heart's ability to pump normally, which can weaken the organ and cause a backup of fluid into the lungs.

heart-lung machine: A device that temporarily takes over the functions of the heart and lungs during heart surgery.

high blood pressure: An unhealthful condition in which the flow of blood against the walls of the arteries is more forceful than normal.

LDL (low-density lipoprotein): Of the two main types of cholesterol, the "bad cholesterol."

lipoproteins: Small protein packages that carry cholesterol through the bloodstream.

myocardial infarction: The technical term for a heart attack.

plaque: An accumulation of cholesterol and other fatty substances inside one or more arteries.

stent: A small tube inserted into a blocked artery to hold it open, allowing normal blood flow.

stroke: Damage to the brain caused by insufficient blood flow to that organ.

ORGANIZATIONS TO CONTACT

American College of Cardiology (ACC)

Heart House
2400 N Street, NW
Washington, DC 20037
phone: 202-375-7000
website: www.cardiosource.org
e-mail: resource@acc.org

The ACC works to transform cardiovascular care and improve heart health through research, education, and quality care and health policy.

American Heart Association

7272 Grenville Avenue
Dallas, TX 75231
phone: 1-800-242-8721
website: www.heart.org/HEARTORG
e-mail: review.personal.info@heart.org

The oldest voluntary organization in the United States devoted to fighting cardiovascular disease and stroke provides science-based treatment guidelines to healthcare professionals and educates lawmakers and other policymakers, as well as the general public, about heart disease.

Cardiovascular Research Foundation (CRF)

111 East 59th Street
New York, NY 10022
phone: 646-434-4500
e-mail: info@crf.org

The CRF works to improve the survival and quality of life of people with cardiovascular disease through research and education, and it advances the development of safe, effective treatments.

Centers for Disease Control and Prevention (CDC) Division for Heart Disease and Stroke Prevention

4770 Buford Highway, NE
Mail Stop F-72
Atlanta, GA 30341
phone: 1-800-232-4636
website: www.cdc.gov/heartdisease

The CDC works to protect Americans from health safety and security threats and brings new knowledge of health issues, including ailments such as heart disease.

National Heart, Lung, and Blood Institute (NHLBI) Health Information Center

P.O. Box 30105
Bethesda, MD 20824
phone: 301-592-8573
email: NHLBIinfo@nhlbi.nih.gov
website: www.nhlbi.nih.gov/health/infoctr

The NHLBI does research into the causes, prevention, and treatment of cardiovascular disease and fosters the discovery of new knowledge about heart failure, heart attack, high blood pressure, stroke, and related conditions.

Women's Heart Foundation (WHF)

P.O. Box 7827
West Trenton, NJ 08628
phone: 609-771-9600
website: www.womensheart.org
e-mail: bonnie@womensheart.org

The WHF is dedicated to preventing heart disease through education, advocacy, and creating prevention projects. The organization also promotes excellent health-care of women.

Books

American Heart Association. *American Heart Association Low-Salt Cookbook*. New York: Clarkson Potter, 2011. High salt intake is a risk factor for high blood pressure, which is in turn a risk factor for heart disease. This entertaining cookbook offers all sorts of ideas for making tasty dishes with little or no salt.

Michael Chizner. *Clinical Cardiology Made Ridiculously Simple*. Miami: Medmaster, 2013. A cardiologist presents a simple but extremely informative introduction to the subject.

Marc Gillinov and Steven Nissen. *Heart 411: The Only Guide to Heart Health You'll Ever Need*. New York: Three Rivers Press, 2012. As the title implies, this is a comprehensive overview of the heart and the many diseases that can affect it.

Shyla T. High. *Why Most Women Die: How Women Can Fight Their #1 Killer: Heart Disease*. Deadwood, OR: Jackpot Press, 2013. A cardiologist explains why heart disease is no less a threat to women as it is to men in a well-written and easy-to-read book.

Martin S. Lipsky et al. *American Medical Association Guide to Preventing and Treating Heart Disease*. New York: Wiley and Sons, 2008. One of the best general overviews of the heart and heart disease available.

Mayo Clinic. *Healthy Heart for Life!* New York: Time Home Entertainment, 2012. The prominent nonprofit medical group dedicated to both care and research created this very easy-to-read volume about heart disease, accompanied by many colorful photos, diagrams, drawings, and charts.

Michael Ozner. *The Complete Mediterranean Diet: Everything You Need to Know to Lose Weight and Lower Your Risk of Heart Disease*. Dallas: BenBella, 2014. The Mediterranean diet is the most recommended by heart doctors and researchers. A cardiologist explains why and provides sample recipes.

James M. Rippe. *Heart Disease for Dummies*. New York: Wiley, 2012. Although the title makes it sound silly, this book is far from it. The author, a cardiologist, provides a treasure trove of accurate information in a very easy-to-follow format.

Sarah Samaan. *Best Practices for a Healthy Heart*. New York: The Experiment, 2011. The co-director of the Women's Cardiovascular Institute delivers an easy-to-read, well-organized look at heart disease and its risk factors, symptoms, and treatments. Her chapter on proper diet to prevent heart disease is especially recommended.

Internet Sources

American Heart Association. "What are the Warning Signs of Heart Attack? (www.heart.org/HEARTORG /Conditions/What-Are-the-Warning -Signs-of-Heart-Attack_UCM _308868_Article.jsp). An organization dedicated to heart-related research and health lists the symptoms of an impending heart attack. The site also contains links to other heart-related issues.

Centers for Disease Control and Prevention. "Heart Disease Facts." (www .cdc.gov/heartdisease/facts.htm). The national public health institute of the United States presents basic facts and statistics about heart disease and heart attacks in the United States each year.

National Heart, Lung, and Blood Institute. "What is Coronary Artery Bypass Grafting?" (www.nhlbi.nih .gov/health/health-topics/topics /cabg). One of the centers that make up the U.S. government agency responsible for biomedical and health-related research provides a detailed overview of the most common surgery for cardiovascular disease—a bypass operation.

PBS Online. "Timeline: The Heart in History." (www.pbs.org/wgbh/amex /partners/breakthroughs/b_history .html.) As part of a multimedia website related to the documentary film *Partners of the Heart*, the U.S. public television network PBS provides this fascinating look at what people knew about the heart and heart health at various points in history.

INDEX

Diabetes, 26, 38–39, 62, 68, 75, 84
Diet. *See specific diets and nutrition elements*

E

Endocarditis, 16
EKG (electrocardiogram), 47, 48–51, *50*, *51*
Exercise
  cardiovascular disease and, 15, 23, 62–65, 75, 90
  against obesity, 38, 60, 79
  importance of physical activity, 62–65, *64*
  stress tests, 51–52

F

Fiber (dietary), 25–26, *83*, 83–84
Framingham Heart Study, 24

G

Gated blood pool scans, 55
Gender differences with cardiovascular disease, 11–12, 39
Genetic risk factors, 38–40

H

Heart
  artificial, *72*, 72–73
  development of medical understanding of, 19–24, *23*
  early human understanding of, 17–19, *18*
  key role, 28
  medications, 67–69
  structure, 20, *21*
Heart attacks
  cardiac arrest, 41
  CT scan for, 53
  defined, 14–16, *15*
  overview, 40–43

scar tissue from, 53–54
  statistics, 16–17
  symptoms, 46–47, *47*
Heart bypass surgery, 70–71
Heart disease. *See* Cardiovascular disease
Heart transplants, *23*, 24, 71
Heart-lung machine, 71
High blood pressure
  cardiovascular disease and, 10, 26, 28, 41
  heart-healthy diet against, 75, 85–86
  medications, 67–68
  normal pressure, 29
  obesity and, 36–38

L

L-carnitine, 82–83
Liver (organ), 30, 73, 87

M

Mediterranean diet, *80*, 81–83, 84–86, 90
MRI (magnetic resonance imaging), 55–57, *56*
Myocardial infarction. *See* Heart attack

O

Obesity
  cardiovascular disease and, 25–26
  high blood pressure and, 36–38
  ideal weight, 76–79, *77t*
Olive oil, 84–86, *85*
Open-heart surgery, 7, 69–71, *70*

P

Pericarditis, 16
Plaque buildup, 13–14, 23, *30*, 31, *31*

R

Red meat and health, 82
Red wine, *87*, 87–88

S

Salt intake, 82
Scar tissue from heart attack, 53–54
Secondhand smoke, 33–36, *34*, 60
Seven Countries Study, 80
Smoking
    avoiding/quitting, 60–62, 63
    cardiovascular disease from, 31–33
    teens and, *32, 61*
Stem cells, 73–74
Stents, 69
Stress management, 65–67, *66*
Stress tests, 51–52, *52*

Stroke, 41–42, *42*
Support groups, *66*, 66–67

V

Vitamins and heart health, 7, 75

W

Western diet, 81

X

X-rays, 48–53, 55

PICTURE CREDITS

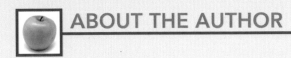
ABOUT THE AUTHOR

In addition to his numerous acclaimed volumes on ancient civilizations, historian Don Nardo has published several studies of modern scientific and medical discoveries and phenomena. Among these are *Germs, Atoms, Biological Warfare, Eating Disorders, Sleep Problems, Vaccines, Malnutrition, DNA Forensics,* and biographies of scientists Charles Darwin and Tycho Brahe. Nardo lives with his wife Christine in Massachusetts.